RINGCRAFT

The Deluxe Edition

JIM DRISCOLL

Featherweight Champion of the World

Promethean Press

Ringcraft: The Deluxe Edition

Promethean Press
PO Box 5572
Frisco, TX 75035
www.promethean-press.com

Manufactured in the United States of America

ISBN 978-0-9810202-1-1

TABLE OF CONTENTS

FOREWORD

Peerless Jim Driscoll was the master of defence and the master of the straight left. Many of his opponents would find themselves chasing his shadow as he effortlessly dodged the best they could offer.

Born in the docks area of Cardiff, Wales in 1880, Driscoll was one of five children, losing their father in an accident when Jim was only seven month's old.

As with many boxers at the time, Jim Driscoll began learning his trade in the boxing booths. Fighting against anyone, rumour has it; he would challenge anyone to hit him on the nose as he stood on a handkerchief with his hands tied round his back.

In 1906, he fought against the British Featherweight Champion Joe Bowker. With the fight going the full fifteen rounds, Driscoll's superiority overpowered Bowker and he won on a points decision. Driscoll inexplicable gave up his title and in the following year; he met Bowker again, this time knocking him out in the seventeenth round to become champion for the second time.

A year later, Driscoll avenged his only defeat to date, beating Harry Mansfield in 6 rounds and then defeating Charles Griffin for the Empire title.

By now, Driscoll's reputation had crossed the Atlantic and America began calling. Just before he left for America, he promised, upon his return, he would fight in an exhibition bout for the Nazareth House Orphanage Annual Charity Show.

In America at the time, no-decisions were the order of the day and the rules stated that if a fighter wasn't knocked out, the fight would be declared a no-decision. This was the primary reason that prevented Driscoll being crowned a World Champion.

In February 1910, Driscoll fought Abe Attell, the World Featherweight Champion in a ten round no-decision contest, the only contest to which Attell would actually agree.

Jim's constant straight left and ring craft took the match to the distance but as this was a no-decision bout, no fighter could be declared the winner though for betting purposes, the ringside reporters gave the result to Driscoll. Driscoll was offered a rematch but declined, to honour the promise he made to the Nazareth House Orphanage. Being a gentleman true to his word, Driscoll passed up the opportunity for a second shot at the world title.

Driscoll was presented with the first Featherweight Lord Lonsdale belt, defeating Seaman Hayes in 6 rounds and once again becoming British Featherweight Champion. Later that year he fought Freddie Welsh but with him becoming extremely agitated at Welsh's holding and kidney punches, Driscoll's temper boiled over and he butted Welsh full in the face, being immediately disqualified by the referee.

In his next fight, Driscoll defeated Spike Robson in seven rounds, giving him the first ownership of a Lord Lonsdale belt.

After the First World War broke out, Driscoll joined the Armed Forces and did not fight for six years.

After a couple of comeback fights, Jim stepped in the ring to fight Charles Ledoux, a fighter considered to be the best featherweight fighter in the world at the time. It was not the best decision Driscoll ever made, owing to him being eleven years older than Ledoux and being taken ill four days prior to the match.

Nevertheless, the bout took place and Driscoll climbed into the ring a sick man, looking grey and haggard. However when the fight started, Driscoll came to life, hitting Ledoux at will, dancing, bobbing, weaving, feigning, jabbing - displaying all of his old ring craft for fifteen rounds. In the eighth round even Ledoux joined in with the audience's applause.

Sadly towards the end of round fifteen, Driscoll became tired and Ledoux landed a wild right to Driscoll's body. Had he followed up, the fight would have ended there but due to Ledoux's surprise at actually connecting, the bell was rung. Driscoll's corner tried to bring him round and tried to convince him to walk away but he wasn't having any of that. The bell was rung for the sixteenth round, Driscoll staggered to his feet and before a punch could be thrown, Jim's corner threw in the towel.

Several years later on January 30, 1925, Peerless Jim Driscoll passed away. At his funeral, over 100,000 people lined the street of his hometown, proving the high respect that people had for him. One hundred children from the Nazareth House Orphanage led the procession.

In 1997, a statue was erected in his honour near the Central Boys Club, where he trained. A Street in Cardiff has also been named after him - Jim Driscoll Way.

Carl Fox
Leeds Martial Arts

Chapter One

The Supreme Importance of Ringcraft

When the average amateur joins the professional ranks, he usually does so filled with hope and radiant dreams of the prosperity and fame which he fondly anticipates will fall to his lot. This is particularly the case when he has achieved any considerable success" as an amateur. For in that case he has usually put in quite a decent time at sparring or serious practice bouts with his old professional tutor, and plumes himself on the success which has attended his efforts in these trial journeys.

Consequently, he looks forward to a fairly comfortable career in the profession, and is apt to feel bitterly disappointed should he meet with defeat, as is usually the case; when, as often happens, his self-confidence has tempted him to fly at fairly high game.

Much, of course, depends on circumstances. His early professional opponents may be merely rough and ready fighters, whose sole claim to distinction is the ability both to hit hard and to take punishment, and in this case, supposing him to be equally gifted, it is probable that his superior coaching may carry him through successfully.

Early triumphs which may prove a serious handicap to his later career. For, flushed by them, he may imagine himself a world-beater in embryo, and confirm himself in habits, which he will find himself unable to shake off or vary, when opposed to a really formidable opponent.

He may be a smart, clever boxer, quick on his feet and with a respectable punch in either hand; but these qualities, though eminently useful in themselves, should not be depended on solely. The man who would win at boxing, like the man who would win at any other sport or business, must utilise his brain; must plan and contrive and be always ready to adapt his tactics, his fist play, his every motion to the situation in hand.

One style of fighting may carry a man to victory in a dozen contests, and yet may fail utterly when employed on a thirteenth occasion, though the last opponent may very possibly be one who has already succumbed to one or more of the defeated twelve.

I do not say that such would invariably be the case, but it is well within the bounds of possibility.

7

The Virtues and Defects of the Straight Left

Take, for instance, the case of the much and justly praised straight left method of boxing. If one were to listen to a certain school of critics, one would suppose that a boxer had only to cultivate this upstanding, classical style to practically assure himself of success against any and every opponent, save those who had developed greater perfection in it than himself.

I might easily quote instances in support of my argument that the straight left is not everything, but only the beginning of everything; but it would be better, perhaps, to confine ourselves to hypothetical illustration.

Let us imagine, therefore, a lad who has studied and practised the method of boxing always in an upright position, with the left foot advanced, the left arm thrown out loosely. A boxer who relies mainly on his right for parrying, and who is content to depend on left leads for the majority of points he rattles up, and also on a straight left counter as the surest means of stopping or checking an onrushing opponent.

It may at once be conceded that this is far and away the best style of boxing. The man who relies on the straight left, on the good old English style, that is to say, has already set his feet on the road to success. He may travel that path by other methods, but other things being equal, he will travel more swiftly by this one.

But he must not fall into the error of imagining that the straight left alone will carry him any great distance.

I have known boxers, and my readers must know many others, who have been very smart in the use of that weapon, and who have been written down as champions accordingly, but who have yet proved very second-rate articles indeed, when they ran up against opponents who, though they might be far inferior in style and method, yet were sufficiently skillful tacticians to force their way in to close quarters, where their own rougher, two-handed methods could be brought to bear.

For the vast majority of the "schooled" boxers, the men, that is to say, who have learnt their boxing from instructors, and on what is known as the *right, correct* lines, and who have consequently become proficient in the use of the left hand, appear to become wedded to the belief that that hand and that hand alone, can safe-

Stepping back to a left lead and shooting a left counter to the chin.

ly be depended upon as an offensive weapon.

It is very natural that they should do so by the way. For the men they will have practised with, and the majority of the men whom they have met in competition, together with the judges who have adjudicated, have been possessed mainly of the same ideas.

Several of their opponents will, of course, depend more on right-handed deliveries than they do themselves. But they will all have been taught, more or less religiously, to look upon the left as *the* weapon, and will on that account be more liable to fall a victim to it. Few amateur boxers appear to have studied or practised methods of avoiding or breaking past a left-handed opposition, while as amateur competitions consist almost solely of three-round bouts, the contestants are all in such a hurry to run up as many points as they can, as quickly as possible, that far too little attention is devoted to the practice of moves, whereby an opponent's strong points may be either negatived or else turned against himself.

An amateur bout is a much faster affair, as a rule, than the average lower grade professional contest, for the simple reason that the men who take part in the latter mentioned, are habituated to six, eight, or even ten round engagements, and are thus in by no means so great a hurry to get home a telling punch or so, which will give them an advantage in the first one or two rounds. They know that they have time at their disposal, and can, therefore, afford to devote some of it to weighing their men up.

The three round man will go up, stand toe-to-toe and do his best to score at once. He has formed a plan beforehand, or is absolutely planless, and in either case rarely dreams of altering his initial tactics, when he discovers them to be unsuccessful. He hasn't the time, for one thing, or rather cannot bring himself to believe that he has. The whole of the first round may have gone before he satisfies himself that he isn't doing as well as he might. Whereupon he determines to infuse a lot more energy into his actions, and to rely rather upon strength and resolution than upon generalship.

The fact is that he feels he cannot afford to experiment. The first round has proved unpropitious, but not so absolutely disastrous, perhaps, as to deprive him of all hope for the next two, supposing them to be fought on the same lines, which naturally happen to be (on his part) the method he knows best. A change to

Stopping a left swing for the face and
sending a straight left to the chin.

another style of attack (supposing him to possess one) will almost certainly be a change to something with which he is less familiar, and concerning which he must on that account feel somewhat doubtful.

Really, he dare not risk going for his man in a different way, and must, therefore, abandon all attempt at cultivating one of the most important sections of ringcraft or ring generalship.

Of course, I do not wish it to be thought that I am saying that the above is invariably the case, but rather that it is so in the generality of instances, as could be proved by many examples.

To take only one. Not so very many years ago, a certain highly successful amateur boxer joined the professional ranks. He had won the highest honours possible, and had proved himself to be at least a street in front of every other amateur in his division, so that he could reasonably anticipate doing fairly well in his new calling, and it may at once be confessed that his career up to date looks like amply fulfilling, if not well exceeding, its promise.

Many very competent critics, indeed, have gone so far as to predict the very highest honours for him, and their prophecies would appear to be by no means ill-founded.

But he will have to learn a lot more about ringcraft before he can travel any great distance. Just at present one might almost say that he will have to begin to learn about ringcraft. For, honestly, he knows very little.

In his very first professional battle he met a far inferior boxer, a man with every physical disadvantage in height, reach, etc., and yet a man who, despite the fact that he was out-pointed in the vast majority of rounds, not only always threatened danger, but actually nearly put the ex-amateur out on more than one occasion.

Our ex-amateur boxed magnificently. He was cool and steady, but he showed that he knew practically next to nothing about infighting, and, worse still, had but one method of stopping his opponent from coming in to him.

Whenever the experienced professional rushed, he simply shot out his left. Usually, so well and forcibly did he direct this that he caught his man in full stride, checked him, and shook him badly.

The professional himself was not remarkably wily, and was, therefore, usually content to rush with the idea of ducking that left, and when he succeeded in doing so, was frequently able to get home a swinging right, which shook the classical boxer up badly. Then, again, the latter had his man beaten to the world at a comparatively early stage, but did not know how to finish him. The professional saved himself very pluckily and recovered, to lose the verdict, of course, but with the gratification that he had not only stayed the journey, but had earned a lot of credit by his very gallant display.

Meeting another opponent later on, after achieving one or two more victories, our ex-amateur displayed no symptom of having developed his ringcraft. He again boxed beautifully, and, being faced by a man who was at even greater physical disadvantages, etc., than his previous opponents, would have been expected to score a fairly easy victory.

But this man soon tumbled to that straight left, ducked under it cleverly and varying his mode of attack had by far the best of the exchanges. The verdict was given a draw, but the ex-amateur was lucky in getting off so cheaply. He was the better boxer and the stronger man, but was out-generalled during two-thirds of the bout, having his much longer reach and greater height chiefly to thank for the points he was able to make.

He commenced well, and was forging comfortably ahead during the first few rounds, but had only one style of boxing. This paid until his opponent varied his method of attack, when he was immediately puzzled. He gallantly pegged away in the old sweet manner, and is to be complimented on his doggedness. But he will do well to learn that gallantry and a straight left are not the only essentials to success in the boxing profession.

How Champions are Cultivated

I have dealt at considerable length with the case of the well known amateur turning professional, for, despite many opinions and much experience to the contrary, the ex-amateur champion, or, at all events, the amateur who has achieved fame, is the very man who ought to make a name for himself as a professional.

James J. Corbett, Jimmy Britt, Eddie McGoorty, Johnny Condon, Harry Thomas, to mention only a few, were all distinguished amateurs before they took to boxing as a profession, while Bob Fitzsimmons stepped straight into an amateur championship competition, won it, and then marched right on to the defeat of five big professionals on the same evening in one tournament, one of the men he met being the famous Maori, Herbert Slade, who two years later was thought good enough to match against John L. Sullivan.

In a sense, of course, every professional must commence as an amateur, but the majority of professionals make their first public appearances as paid men.

They may have previously joined a boxing club and so acquired the rudiments of boxing either from an instructor or by sparring among themselves, but their knowledge is usually of a very rough and ready sort, and their first valuable lessons are those learnt in actual conflict at boxing booths or small shows where money prizes are given.

Take my own case, for instance. I was employed as a boy in the printing and publishing department of the *Western Mail*, Cardiff, where, of course, we boys used to fight pretty often among ourselves. We had no idea about boxing, but just used to set about each other whenever we quarrelled, putting in all we knew, and being very often far too excited and indignant to think about science or tactics, even if we had known what those words meant.

But there was one smart boy who did fancy himself as a boxer. I believe he had received a few lessons, and had had some practice with the gloves, so that he was very anxious to make himself recognised as the cock of the walk among us.

I don't quite remember now how it came about, but this boy and I were always coming into conflict. We had three or four rough and tumbles, of which I had the better, and I suppose this worried him.

He wanted to get his own back, and when a boxing competition for boys under 7 stone was arranged at a public hall in Cardiff, he fancied he saw his chance. He could box, or thought he could, and he was quite sure that I knew nothing about boxing; so if he could only persuade me to enter, and could manage to meet me in one of the rounds - well, there was all the revenge he wanted.

So he and his father waylaid me as I was going home that night and told me all about this tournament. They wouldn't let me go, badgering me to enter, until I consented, and then marched me under their escort straight to the hall.

I don't know how and didn't trouble at the time, but they worked

Stopping a man with a sraight left to the face

the thing all right, up to a certain stage. He and I met that same night in a bout, and it was a bout, they tell me.

There wasn't much boxing about it, you understand. He may have been very expert with the gloves, but I didn't give him any time to make use of his cleverness. Just went at him, with both arms whirling and chased him about all over the stage.

I won the competition, too, in the end, and got a few shillings for my trouble, a result which struck me as very remarkable. Because, you see, I had been enjoying the fun, and it was quite a new experience to get paid for amusing myself.

Soon after that they had an amateur competition for 9 stone boys (I think it was) which I entered for and won, and then another for 8 stone lads. I suppose that I ought to have been barred from entering either, as I had already received money for boxing, but no one raised any objection, and, as a matter of fact, the only amateur element in those competitions was the prize. This was a solid silver cup worth £5, or some similar sum. The sort of article, you know, which you have to struggle hard to pawn for one shilling if you want to raise money on it.

However, I won two of these cups and a gold (?) watch as well, in another competition I went in for. So I was quite satisfied that this boxing game was the thing which suited me down to the ground. I thought it worth paying a lot of attention to, and I was giving my mind seriously to it. But all the time, I was only just a kid, who wanted to earn as much pocket money as he could. I wasn't thinking about becoming a champion, either of England or of the world at that time, but was just boxing because I liked it and because I was picking up stray prizes and small sums of money, which either looked pretty on the mantelpiece at home or else came in useful in many ways.

Pedlar Palmer then came down to Wales running tournaments and getting up competitions, and as I won several of these, people began to talk about me, and I got matched for one or two contests - and, well, I suppose you know the rest.

I have told all this just because it illustrates, in the clearest manner I can think about, the usual process by which the average boxer gets manufactured. He just takes to the business like a young duck taking to water, knowing very little about the fine points of the game, but picking them up as he goes along. His only

Feinting a man to get him to lead for the face.

instructor is actual experience, and this after all is, I suppose, the best. At all events, it is the one which most impresses the novice.

But then, on the other hand, the process is to some extent rather a slow one. I suppose that I ought to plead guilty to having been exceptionally lucky, inasmuch as the men I met were always just a shade inferior to me. Of course, I watched all the boxing I could, just as I watch it now, and in my earlier days was always discovering why men did this and that and picking up all the wrinkles I could.

Had I had the misfortune to run up against a really superior man in those days, I might have had to take a severe beating, and might in consequence have lost confidence and got discouraged, while had I again, on the other hand, always had easy journeys, I might have got satisfied that I knew all that there was to be known and that I need not trouble to try and improve myself.

But, as it happened, many of my early opponents gave me stiff battles, and so forced me to get thinking. I was always anxious to finish things as quickly as I could, and to, as far as possible, avoid getting hurt myself, and these two anxieties of mine made me plan and contrive and take notice of how cleverer and more experienced men than myself managed to do the things I wanted to do.

But every boxer is not likely to be equally fortunate, and I would not like to say that this crude system is the best which could be pursued.

It is the method which used to be employed in practically every branch of athletics, and one which used formerly to work well with runners, footballers, wrestlers, and athletes of every description. But it is getting superseded today, when so many, men are taken in hand and carefully trained and practised as soon as they show signs of possessing any great capacity. The self-made boxer will, of course, always be found round about the top, for the simple reason that he has a natural gift and love for the game. If he did not possess these qualities, he would soon drop out, but, having them, he forces his way to the front in spite of all the obstacles in his path.

But, he is likely to find things far more difficult in future. The profession is becoming much more attractive than it used to be. There are bigger prizes to be won, and many more of them. Even a fourth or fifth rater can today pick up a fairly decent living, if he only looks after himself and does not waste his earnings. So that,

Ducking a left lead and driving the left to the body.

as a result, the new men who enter the ranks will study things. They will spare no trouble to obtain the best instruction obtainable, and as this will make the profession of instructor far more lucrative than it has been in the past, the instruction obtainable will naturally improve.

It would not be such a wild prophecy, indeed, to assert that many men will take up amateur boxing as a sort of trial trip, or, shall we say, as a university course, and then "passed with honours," adopt the profession in all seriousness. One has only to remember the enormous purses which are being so freely offered for championship contests today, to realise that a much better educated class of man than has previously followed the boxing profession will see in it an honourable and profitable career in life, though for the matter of that, the coming generation in every class of life will be much better educated than the present one.

It is impossible, moreover, to avoid acknowledging that of late years the majority of international contests between English and American boxers have resulted in favour of the latter, and that (despite the fact that here and there we have men well able to hold their own with the very best men the United States can produce), the general level of boxing in America is of a far higher standard than it is with us.

Our very best men find it very difficult to keep busy in their own country, for the simple reason that there is such a dearth of opponents of their own calibre. Yet they have but to cross the Atlantic, no matter what their weight or class may be, to find as many matches as they want.

There are many reasons for this, one, of course, being that the boxing game has for many years been far more profitable and popular in America than it has been with us.

But the chief reason, for which the preceding is only a cause, is that the mass of American boxers are, as a rule, a more intelligent and self-respecting class than their British confreres. Not that the British boxer is to blame for his inferiority in these respects. His has been a somewhat precarious existence, and he, himself, has been regarded in many quarters as a pariah, only allowed to breathe on sufferance and totally unworthy of any righteous man's consideration.

Consequently, he has been a somewhat humble individual,

whose aspirations and ambitions have been nipped in the bud, He loses the habit of asserting himself, and when he runs up against an American, who struts into the ring, with an all-conquering air, which, by the way, has been his leading characteristic throughout all the preliminary negotiations, and who in dress, manner, and behaviour has generally endeavoured to impress the Briton with a sense of his (the Yank's) infinite superiority in every respect - social, physical and mental; he is a beaten man before the gong has gone for the first round.

This last-mentioned business, by the way, is a little piece of that preliminary ringcraft which the average American so sedulously cultivates.

But boxing contests, after all, are decided in the ring itself, and it is the generalship which is then employed which will decide the issue.

A man may win his fight by superior boxing science or by greater punching power, but unless he get home a lucky blow or be vastly superior in the former quality, he cannot hope to hold his own against a really clever ring strategist who will know how to minimise his rival's natural advantages, and possibly even to utilise them as weapons for that rival's undoing.

It is the man who realises that boxing contests are more readily won by brains than by fists who is going to make a world's champion, and I would ask my readers to remember that although the hints given in the following chapters will be (I hope) found useful, that their usefulness will depend chiefly on the discretion with which they are employed.

It is rare, indeed, to meet a couple of boxers, consecutively, who can be beaten by the employment of exactly the same methods, and it is, therefore, essential that one should be always prepared to vary one's tactics not only for individual opponents, but also to vary them at different stages of most combats.

In my own early days, when I did a lot of boxing at fairs and other places, travelling round with a boxing booth and taking on all comers, I suppose that I had about the best possible schooling in this respect. It is true, of course, that the majority of my opponents were of the very rough-and-ready type, whose notions of boxing were chiefly confined to hard punching, and who possessed little acquaintance with the finer points of the game, but these adversaries were none the less formidable on that account. One had to be prepared for any and every sort of blow, coming from every conceivable angle and at all sorts of unorthodox moments. Now and again one ran up against really clever men as well, but it was rarely that these gave one so much anxiety as the "sloggers." One's experience was of little use against these latter gentry, because their method of fighting could seldom be anticipated with any degree of accuracy.

This booth boxing was a roughish school, perhaps, but it was undoubtedly the best then obtainable, and (save for the exacting nature of the work involved) I am not so sure that it was not the very best possible preparation I could possibly have had for a career which has not been altogether unsuccessful. For, not only did I learn how to take care of myself against some of the hardest and most determined opponents one could wish to meet, but, what was of far greater importance, the best and surest method of conserving one's energy.

Pretty nearly everyone of these booth contests was of the briefest possible description, it is true, but then I would often meet as many as six or seven different opponents in one day, and could never be certain that the most formidable ones might not be the very men who turned up last, and whom, it was desirable, from the booth proprietor's point of view, to dispose of in the shortest possible time.

Chapter Two

A Few
Simple Outlines

Perhaps the best and soundest advice any trainer, second, or other adviser can give his principal concerning a forthcoming contest is that he should make a point of getting to know as much as he possibly can about his prospective opponent.

The best method of doing this is, firstly, to watch him in action, and, secondly, to either discuss his methods with someone who has met him; or, better still, to engage that someone as sparring partner and second. It being always provided that the gentleman in question is a person of observation and common sense.

A man may vary his tactics as much as he likes, but through all his manoeuvres will generally run some recognisable scheme of action. He will have one pet system of attack, which, cloak it as he may, he will usually pursue, and which, if carefully observed, studied and prepared for, can or ought to be utilised for his undoing.

For instance, let us suppose that a man has a fondness for close in-fighting. That is to say, that his forte consists in getting practically body to body, where he can hammer one's ribs, stomach or possibly kidneys. All which blows will possibly only be preliminaries to a sudden whip over for the chin.

You, we will suppose, are rather fond of infighting yourself, and may, therefore, be tempted to let him have his way and come in to you. But, even when you are fairly satisfied that you have a harder body punch than he has, that you protect your own ribs and stomach better, and that you can ram in half-arm deliveries both faster and with more telling effect, it is by no means always the wisest course to let your opponent have his way with you.

You have only surmised that you are a better in-fighter than he is, an opinion in which you may find yourself mistaken, while even if in the first two or three rallies of that description you are able to prove your superiority, it is by no means impossible that your opponent will also become convinced of the fact, and will, in consequence, make a complete change in his tactics, and prefer rather to out-fight you, with the possible result that he may prove a better long range boxer, even than you are yourself.

It must be admitted that there is a lot of supposition about all this, but it is just as well to bear all these facts in mind before deciding on the best plan of campaign against such a man as we have imagined.

Now, a man such as this, who is rather fond of coming in close, will almost certainly try to do so, if you lead him to think that you are not particularly keen on that mode of fighting. But your actual desire is to get him to come at you and to get him to do so in such fashion as will permit of your dealing out some really serious damage, whenever he makes the attempt.

You can shake him up pretty badly by so doing, and can then join issue with him at the in-fighting game, if you so desire, with a fair amount of confidence, because you know that you have taken most of the steam out of him, and may, therefore, be certain instead of hopeful that you will be able to punch him both harder and faster at close quarters.

Spar at him, therefore, first, and display a decided disinclination to mix things. Keep leading at him lightly with your left, but without committing yourself to really definite blows, seeking rather to tap him than to hurt. Should you be so fortunate as to possess a longer reach, you should by these tactics commence to run up a decent score of points, and in any case irritate him somewhat. He will become more or less convinced that you are more than half afraid of him, and if you, as you should, pay particular attention to your defence, you will be able to avoid his getting home on you with any effect.

Rely extensively on footwork. Don't mind retreating if he shows a disposition to force matters, and concentrate all your attention on preserving a respectable distance between yourself and him.

He won't be able to stand this sort of thing long, and sooner or later will be almost certain to make a desperate effort to get to closer quarters, where his favourite hook blows or half-arm jabs can have their effect.

He may, of course, try to force his way in, by sheer weight of metal, but you will or should have convinced him already that should he try this method, you will make him pay very dearly for so attempting and that your left hand can interpose a barrier which is not to be circumvented in a hurry. For it must not be imagined that my criticism of the habit of relying solely on the straight left style of fighting was in any way intended to minimise the prime importance of cultivating, and, if possible, perfecting this branch of boxing. The

Stopping a right swing for the jaw and sending the right to the chin.

two-handed and crouching styles of attack have been much belauded by some critics, but the good old English method, as perfected by Jem Mace, will always beat any other position or style.

Stand well upright always, make the best use of such inches as you have, and throw the left out. Don't, however, get into the habit of imagining that the right is either the only defensive weapon or that it is to be used as a shield alone. You will probably carry a better punch in it than you do in your left, but even if you don't, you will find the right a most useful weapon of offence, whereas your left will be primarily more valuable for the purpose of keeping opponents at a distance.

Let it always preserve the straight line and keep it, as general rule, usually directed at the other fellow's face, when you will find that he will be forced to duck and come in head down if he wants to get in at you.

Prod away at him and break ground a trifle at each of his attempts to force his way in, until you compel him to lower his head and charge, when you ought really to have him at your mercy.

Of course, if he is a wise man, he will endeavour to come with his head under your left, shooting a left jab for your body as he comes, because, by so doing, he will take his face out of the road of a right upper cut, and as this is the precise blow which you have been aiming, all along, to get home, you must always be prepared for this style of attack.

Just at first, you will rely mainly on previous observation of his methods and, to some extent, on instinct, as a guide to his exact method of procedure; but you should not find it so overwhelmingly difficult to meet his charge with a straight right upward jab. The slightest turn to the left, as he comes, will bring you again face to face, if he tries to tuck his head out of danger on that side, and you will usually find that a stiff bent arm upper cut will prove more effective than a swinging one.

For one thing, the aim can be better directed, and, for another, the effect will be more jarring. A good deal will depend on circumstances here, but it will generally be found that another short step backwards the moment your upper cut has gone, will give you an opening to get in another, while, should your adversary prove particularly strong, and his rush very determined, you may by continuing your retreat even get three or four home.

Should you utilize the bent arm stiff upper jab, it is best to aim at the face, and, preferably, the chin, where the blow will have its greatest effect. But then, it may be objected, the other fellow may carefully cover his face up when he rushes, as Freddie Welsh does, for instance; in which case your upper cut won't be likely to find the target you have discharged it at. Well, this is, of course, one of those cases for which you should have prepared yourself by previous observation, and, any way, you will not be meeting gentlemen of that quality until you get up among the champions.

Boxers of average ability, when they cover up their faces and rush in are rarely, if ever, able to perform both feats satisfactorily. Either the face is left very imperfectly guarded, or else the *rush* can only be so described by courtesy. Direction and pace will probably both be sacrificed to the crouch and cover.

Still, when a man does make even an imperfect cover; there is always the probability that the jab, previously recommended, may meet his gloves instead of his face, and unless one be very certain of one's aim, the swinging upper cut for the body is to be preferred. The resultant effect may not be quite as telling, but it is nevertheless an unpleasant blow to receive.

Now, having coaxed your man into attacking you in this fashion, and having, as you calculated on doing, upper cut him with effect, beware of standing off to admire your handiwork. Quite a number of boxers commit this fault, and thereby throwaway contests which should have resulted in victories for them.

A Golden Rule

It may be as well at this stage to remark that there is one precept a boxer should never forget, and that is that he should never waste a moment between gong and gong. He is there to beat his man, and to beat him as soon as he can. It is very pleasant to feel so confident of your skill, that you are indifferent as to whether the contest goes the specified number of rounds or not, but though you may be satisfied that you are so much the better boxer, that a decision on points can only mean a verdict for yourself, yet it is always as well to remember that accidents have been known to happen, before now.

Quite apart from the fact that the referee may not entertain the same exalted opinion of your skill that you do yourself, there is always the possibility (however remote) that he may commit an error of judgment; while, beside either of these untoward happenings, there is always the yet greater possibility of even a much inferior opponent getting over one of the right sort to the point and thereby robbing you of all further interest in the contest in question. This, moreover, is an accident which may happen at any time, and, above all, may very easily happen when things have been going most remarkably smoothly for you in every respect.

You have been sailing along in the utmost comfort, and have already been tasting your victory, fully confident that you are already enjoying so long a lead that your opponent can by no possibility succeed in evening matters up; and, in these circumstances, it is almost impossible to avoid getting careless. The temptation to "show off " is almost irresistible, especially to a young boxer. He leaves openings, recklessly. The other fellow, supposing him to be a game fellow, is almost in despair. He knows that he hasn't an earthly chance of winning on points, and that he can only succeed by the "knock out route."

Consequently, he risks being served with this sauce himself. He may, possibly, throw his own chances away, by disclosing his hopes. That is to say, he may just come at you furiously, swinging both hands for all he is worth, with the obvious intention of getting one home at all risks. This is, of course, a very foolish method, as it cannot fail to warn the leader, who, unless he is the most obtuse of persons, will thereupon cut out all the gallery tricks and rest content with boxing warily, satisfied with his long lead, and resolved only to keep his own end up, or to increase it gradually by letting go only when he knows that he can do so with absolute security to himself.

But the cool, steady boxer, who knows that the tide is running steadily against him, will work for that knock out for all he is worth. He will even sham greater grogginess than he feels (of which more later), and will watch with eagle eyes for the chance of one slam at an uncovered jaw. There have been quite a number of occasions on which the issue has been reversed at the very last moment, and it is possible that not a few readers will recall the very sensational finish to the contest between Tom Ireland and Darkey Wallace at the National Sporting Club on March 28, 1898, when the former,

Pressing on a covered-up man's gloves in order to coax them higher and then uppercutting with a right to the chin.

the easiest winner imaginable on points, was put down and out in the 20th round, with barely 20 seconds to go before the final gong.

For which reasons it is always advisable to glue your eyes on your opponent even at the cost of neglecting to watch the signals of your seconds. For, when all is said and done, these last-mentioned aids to success are not of the very first importance. I am not saying that even a champion may not at times receive a useful hint from his corner during the course of a round, but even he should be able to dispense with such as a rule, while it is far better as a general principle to rely almost entirely on one's own observation. Listen always to the recommendations of your adviser or advisers, during the minute interval, and act upon them if they appeal to your judgment, or, in the event of your esteeming their opinion as superior to yours, even *against* your judgment in critical situations, though this latter piece of advice is given with considerable hesitation and with the reservation that the state of affairs must be indeed desperate before it should be accepted as a maxim.

A champion, or, at all events, a first-rate boxer, should be clever enough to spare an eye for his corner without unduly exposing himself, but a novice or a man of comparatively little experience would do well to refrain from even casting a glance in that direction, save when he is in a clinch, with his chin resting fairly securely on his opponent's shoulder, or is otherwise more or less protected against the risk of a sudden onslaught.

A very considerable number of boxers are far too fond, by the way, of looking round for advice at critical stages of a bout. At certain halls, arenas, or clubs where boxing contests are held, the whole assembly of spectators will sometimes enrol themselves as voluntary additional seconds to one or other of the principals, and spare neither energy nor lung power in tendering their advice to the contestant who has enlisted their sympathies. They will howl advice, abuse, and the most contradictory suggestions to the men engaged, and not infrequently one sees a boxer, confused by the uproar, anxious for victory, and, above all, anxious to please, looking on all sides of him for further hints and instruction. He has got into the habit of doing this through a slavish veneration for the opinion of his official seconds, with the result that he pays as much attention to the crowd as he does to his opponent, the consequences of which it is scarcely necessary to mention.

Watching Your Opponent

To all these reasons it is almost superfluous to add the statement that unless one's adversary be continually surveyed, it is impossible to form any accurate conception either of his plans or of his condition. A clever boxer will at times feign weariness and weakness, for the simple purpose of allowing his opponent to imagine that he can safely allow his attention to wander to his corner or elsewhere, ready the moment he does so to dash in and catch him off his guard. He will also do so for the purpose of tempting him to come in recklessly, with the design of putting a summary finish to the contest, and in so doing forget to guard himself. This, of course, is a very old trick, which one would suppose was familiar to every boxer of any experience, and yet it is really astonishing to notice how frequently it meets with success.

And, by the way, while we are talking of catching a man off his guard, a little reminiscence occurs to me, which, while it has nothing to do with ringcraft, may yet serve to give my readers an idea of the varied kind of opposition which we used to meet in the old boxing booths, to which I have alluded.

There was a certain booth proprietor, who was making a tour of the Welsh fairs, when he happened to visit one at the same time as Frank Craig, the famous "Coffee Cooler." Now Craig, at that time, though somewhat past his best, was still a man of considerable reputation. His fame was widespread, and he might reasonably speculate on achieving a considerable financial success at the fair in question. It was feared by his rivals that he would pack his booth all the time and only leave a residue of spectators for his competitors. Something had to be done and done speedily, so the enterprising showman resolved on a huge piece of bluff.

He had the fortune, good or bad, to come across in his travels a really huge negro, who, having little or no knowledge of boxing, he had engaged as porter, ring attendant, and general handy man. Still, he *looked* a very formidable personage, and the showman relying on the public worship of appearances, billed, him as Frank Craig, the "original Australian Coffee Cooler." That title, and his formidable appearance, did the trick. Garbed in very striking fashion, the negro was instructed to assume a careless attitude outside the booth when he paraded with the other members of the troupe, while the most wonderful challenges were issued on his behalf.

As had been anticipated, the appearance of this "Terror" was enough. The crowd swarmed in to witness the terrible deeds of such a hero, thus leaving the genuine Craig's booth somewhat sparsely attended. The giant's appearance, moreover, was sufficient to scare all opposition away, and though the people came to see him slaughter any rash aspirant who might come along, he was left unmolested to contemplate the deeds of the boxing members of the troupe.

All might have continued to go well, had not a certain big miner, who was pressing forward to get into the booth, unfortunately happened to tread heavily on the imposter's toe. He was profuse in his apologies, but his foot was rather a weighty one, and the big black had become somewhat tickled by the stir he had created. He had actually commenced to believe that he was all that he professed to be, and was feeling rather resentful at being treated solely as an advertising poster. Full of these sentiments, he declined to accept the miner's apologies, and proceeded to threaten to knock his head off, as a punishment for his clumsiness. These threats fired the Celtic blood. "All right," said the Welshman, " I'll have three rounds with you."

The big black's opportunity had come at last. He would now show his boss and the other fellows that he could box just as well as they could, and would, moreover, convince them of what he was already assured, namely, that in him they had a hitherto unsuspected champion of the world. So he promptly entered the booth on the heels of his challenger, and informed his surprised employer that he would personally distinguish himself in the first bout. The showman was in somewhat of a quandary. He had been publicly lamenting the fact that he could find no one brave enough to engage with his star attraction, so could only trust that the miner's courage would ooze away as soon as he found himself face to face with his huge adversary, and meanwhile hoping for the best, expressed his sympathy for the rash fellow who had dared so reckless an enterprise.

Two pairs of gloves were handed out, and the black proceeded leisurely to don his. The miner, however, who was beginning to

Pressing on my opponent's forearms, and in position to whip the right to the face and by slipping off the left as my opponent's right rises to send that hand to the body.

fear the worst; resolved to waste no time in experiencing it. He hurriedly slipped on the right muffler, and then crossing the ring, handed out a tremendous punch to the black, who was still adjusting his "mitts." That fist came home full on the point, and down went the sable hero, and not only did he go down, but he stayed down as well for a full hour or more. It was one of the heaviest and hardest punches I have ever seen delivered. Naturally, there was no little confusion, in the midst of which the miner disappeared.

It was a catastrophe, undoubtedly, but it might easily have been a much more disastrous one. It is true that the reputation of the "Australian Coffee Cooler" had suffered extinction, and that he could no longer be profitably employed as an advertisement, but the sudden nature of his defeat concealed the hollowness of his claims to renown, and any way, he had served his turn.

There is a moral attached to this story, the truth of which has been demonstrated on more than one occasion by American boxers, who, owing to the different custom prevailing in the States, have often been able to catch their British rivals napping. No American boxer, for instance, would ever dream of indulging in that preliminary stroll round the ring which the average Briton appears to regard as the only possible method of commencing a round.

We have adopted the American method of shaking hands and of *then* returning to corners to await the signal to commence, for all battles of the first importance, and there is surely no reason why the custom should not become general.

That absurd and yet solemn walk round at the commencement of each round might be forgiven as forming part of the band shaking ceremony, but when it is repeated after every interval, a lot of time is wasted, which a well-trained boxer might far better employ in disposing of his man. Naturally, one of the first points which every boxer should cultivate sedulously, is the ability to commence briskly, that is to get himself down to work without any delay.

He should always *possess* this quality, though it is not always advisable to make use of it. A sudden, dashing assault will often disconcert an opponent completely, no matter how experienced he, may be, and I may mention here, that Spike Robson almost caught me napping with that wonderful leaping charge of his in the 5th round of our recent contest. I may at once confess that I have never seen anything like it, and though, thanks to my principles, I was watching him very closely, I could never have anticipated his coming at me at the pace he did.

As you will remember, my right eye was closed up, so that my vision was naturally considerably affected, and I caught but the merest glimpse of him as he flew through the air.

Fortunately for me, he stubbed his toe apparently, and, therefore, stumbled. But even this would not have saved me from being driven against my chair and the post, had he let go a left hook instead of a right one when he arrived. That was just where he made the mistake which lost him the fight.

This, by the way, is an admission of what "might have been," for even if he had landed, it is still possible that I might have won. The blow might have proved to be a glancing one, or I might have managed to survive it, but we must in any event have collided, which would have enabled him to escape that collision with my seat, which can by no means have improved his chances. He should have recollected that it was my right eye which was closed, and that I was, therefore, far less able to dodge a blow which was coming from that side. As it was, I was only just able to edge away in time, and he actually brushed me as he passed.

I have dealt with this little incident in detail, because there are so many points in it which the boxer would do well to remember. Robson, I should imagine, fancied that owing to the damaged eye, I was likely to be less formidable for a short time, and that if he could manage to get a really good blow home, the effect might be more than useful. So he came like a thunderbolt, reckless of any and everything, provided he could only get on top of me. Possibly he had formed no plan as to the blow he would deliver when he arrived, but just left that to chance, but as that right of his came round with such ease, force and rapidity, I am more than inclined to fancy that it was the hand he was keeping in readiness, and that although he remembered my eye when planning his ruse, he completely forgot it when thinking about his punch. In short, the rush itself was a magnificent but incompletely conceived piece of ringcraft.

So that here, again, we have one more justification for the word battle when speaking of ring contests. For a boxing contest resembles an actual military battle, inasmuch as both resemble a game of chess. Nothing should be overlooked, no even small item forgotten, and every move should be carefully planned out ahead. The great boxer, like the great chess player, is the man who sees an exchange or so farther ahead than his opponents. He plans to execute such or such a feint, to send over such or such a blow, to side step, retreat, advance or offer his head or body in such or such a manner, simply because he accurately foresees that his opponent will then make a certain reply, which will bring about a particular situation, out of which other situations will or should arise, which will be entirely favourable to the strategist. We are now speaking of course, of the perfect, the ideal boxer, who critics may allege has never yet made his appearance. But then, real success of any description is only achieved by a tentative advance towards the ideal. It may fall a long way below it, perhaps, but then, if it only reaches a shade farther than that made by one's rivals, one is going to get home for the time being.

Quick and Slow Beginners

But, after having pointed out the need for a quick onslaught, which should, at times, resemble a volcanic outburst, it is just as well to remember that this policy will not always pay. A boxer should always cultivate speed above every other quality, save and except stamina, which should, of course, be developed in equal proportion. A big punch is always a singularly useful asset, but it is not the certain winner, though if it gets there, it often proves to be. We must admit that of course. But a man may own the very hardest punch in the world, and yet lose his battles, for the simple reason that owing to his being a slow man, he can only land it on second or third raters.

For which reasons I would strongly recommend you to avoid distressing yourself about any lack of hitting power. Develop it by all means, of course, but avoid doing so at the expense of your speed. Remember that a dozen well aimed and well delivered blows, even though they be of only moderate force, will be quite as, if not immediately so, effective as the heaviest punch one could imagine. Jim Corbett did not beat John L. Sullivan with a single delivery, but with a long succession of them, which continued to land until the Boston giant sank helpless, exhausted, but not knocked out.

Feinting with the left for the body to get a man's guard down and
holding the right in readiness to hit or parry.

Try, therefore, to make yourself the very fastest of your time. You probably will not succeed, but you may become faster than most of your contemporaries. Devote plenty of time to the punch ball, to shadow boxing, and, above all, to sparring practice, with the very fastest partners you can obtain. Never spar lazily, but always insist that your partners shall travel at their very tip-top pace. They may not want to do so; but if you only keep on slamming away at them at your best speed, you will inevitably compel them to join issue with you and so keep level. Should they he unable to last the pace you set them, try and get three of them together and take them on for minute turns without intervals. That is to say, each of them will have two minutes rest per round, while you keep going the whole time, and you will find it no bad plan to devote even the minute interval which you will necessarily allow yourself, to practice with the punch ball. Not invariably, of course, but certainly every now and again. Try four rounds of sparring practice of this description with the intervals occupied by the fastest ball punching you can keep up, for a few days, and you won't have much to complain about either your speed or your staying powers, There is another and equally important reason for developing your speed to the utmost quite apart from its enabling you to surprise your opponents, which I will deal with shortly, but it may be as well to point out why a sudden dashing attack is not invariably advisable.

It is possible, for instance, that you may not be thoroughly acquainted with your opponent. You may be more or less of a stranger to his methods, and you may discover, if you commence straightaway to mix things furiously right from the bell, that you have caught a Tartar; a man, perhaps, who is even fonder of that style of fighting than you are yourself. In which case you will have been playing his game for him, which is the very thing you should avoid doing at all costs.

Feel Your Man Out

Open smartly, therefore, but open always with caution. Leave your chair sharp to the bell and get to the centre of the ring without delay. Strive, indeed, to meet your man half-way or less between his own corner and the centre of the ring, This will curtail the space in which he will have to manoeuvre, and may, perhaps, enable you to drive him back right into his own angle, where you should have matters pretty much your own way. Always be prepared to start in at once, but it is just as well to avoid rushing matters at the start. You may have earned a reputation for so doing, and may, therefore, find him fully prepared to side step anything of this nature. It is best to open with a well-restrained spar, in the course of which you will try every feint that occurs to you as being calculated to coax your man into revealing all his favourite blows. These pet deliveries of his, it should always be remembered, are really his weak points, for the simple reason that he will usually put plenty of force into them and thereby lay himself open to attack when they fail to come off as he has hoped they will.

If you are the practised boxer, I assume that you are, you will naturally be prepared with a useful counter to every blow that is likely to be sent at you, when you have once ascertained what it is likely to be, and as soon as you have discovered your opponent's pet deliveries, you are, or ought to be, in full possession of that little piece of information, because you have simply to invite a blow to feel pretty confident that it will be promptly sent over to you.

Avoid, however, *always* "drawing" these punches. Because, if you do it too often, either your opponent or his seconds will discover your little game and you will then probably discover that all your trouble and labour has been thrown away.

Meanwhile, you have a whole host of other items to discover. You have found out your man's favourite punches, and should at the same time have a pretty shrewd estimate as to his speed.

On Forcing the Pace

If he is a slower man than yourself, you have a fairly simple course of action to pursue. There is nothing which disconcerts a man so much as being compelled to fight out of his stride. He doesn't like it. It confuses him, flurries him, and, above everything else, tires him. There is no necessity to keep rushing at a man in order to achieve this object. Fast feinting and hitting, together with rapid footwork, will do the trick quite as easily, without running you into any risk of getting badly punished in the mix-ups. You may even, if the idea strikes you as being a good one for that particular bout, coax your man into rushing at you, when, if you are quick and smart on your feet, you can lead him a very merry dance all over the ring and tire him out in next to no time.

These, by the way, are the tactics which I pursued in my bout with Seaman Hayes. I knew that I had a hard-hitting, very sturdy and game opponent in front of me. A man who, although he was not a particularly polished boxer, had yet always proved himself to be a very hard nut to crack by some really clever fellows.

I knew and could see that he had been training very hard for this bout, and had even, perhaps, been over-training a trifle. Thinking matters over, I felt pretty certain that he would want to make a slugging match of it. That he would try forcing his way in to me, if possible, to half-arm distance, when he could slog and slam away, more or less indifferent to any punishment he might receive in the process, but resolutely determined on getting home as many hard punches as he could contrive in the earnest hope of getting one "there" which would tell its tale. On the whole, I felt fairly satisfied that he would be very disinclined to let things travel along quietly, at all events at first, and that on the slightest temptation he would come at me for all he was worth.

So it seemed to me that the wisest course I could pursue would be to let him fight just as he wanted to do. Only more so. Yes, he should force the pace, or try to do so, until I had got him travelling much faster than he had ever intended doing.

Among other plans which I formed was a resolution to avoid anything in the nature of a clinch, for at all events as long as I could contrive so to do. Even if Hayes rushed me on to the ropes, or got me into any other temporarily awkward situation, I would seek to escape by ducking and footwork rather than by going into holds. It was an important item of my plan of campaign that the seaman should have as little rest as I could possibly contrive.

In the event, as you may possibly remember, this was exactly what happened. I am not claiming for myself any marvellous ingenuity, but am merely quoting the contest, because it will probably be fairly fresh in your memory and also because it makes a fairly good illustration of the point with which I am dealing. Hayes boxed exactly as I had hoped that he would, and as I had, therefore, planned that he should.

He tore at me right from the outset. I gave back before him as he came on, but only for short distances, just out of the reach of

Getting the inner position and breaking up a man's guard.

his vicious swings and hooks, and no more. He damaged the air pretty considerably, and whenever he showed signs of slackening up, I did my best to get him going again by dabs to the face with either hand. These jolts and dabs of mine were not particularly forcible, but then I did not particularly desire to make them so. Had I been in a hurry to knock Hayes out at short notice, I might very easily have been tempted to join in some slogging rallies, in which the seaman might have succeeded in doing a certain amount of damage, and naturally I had no wish or desire to get hurt more than I could help. There is nothing particularly clever in running any risk of getting beaten yourself when you can, if possible, contrive to win without incurring any such danger.

Besides which I had arranged in my own mind the method in which I hoped to win, or rather had decided on the scheme which I reckoned would enable me to do so most surely, and was, therefore, anxious to guard myself against any temptation to depart from it, so long, of course, as matters were proceeding in a satisfactory fashion for myself.

My main object was to let Hayes beat himself, and so everything I did was carefully calculated to that end. He was in splendid condition, had trained himself most thoroughly, and was famed far and wide as a determined, sturdy fighter with any amount of grit and staying power. And yet, in spite of all these assets, he was puffing and blowing by the end of the first round. I notice, by the way, that the reports mention that in spite of his exertions, Hayes appeared to be quite fresh when he went to his corner, which is really one of the finest testimonials his trainer could wish to receive.

But I had heard him panting and had even noticed that his speed and vigour had lost some of their early force, so, despite his steady and easy step as he walked to his chair, I was satisfied that the pace had begun to tell its tale, and I was, moreover, particularly pleased to notice that its effects were scarcely apparent to others, and (I hoped) to Hayes himself. Because the fitter he deemed himself, the better were my plans suited. I had no desire for any change of tactics on his part, and had, indeed, slightly eased up in the last few seconds for that purpose.

This self-restraint was rewarded in the second round, for Hayes came at me once more as fiercely as before. The rest of the

Another method of breaking up an opponent's guard.

contest needs no relating. He fought with wonderful gameness and pluck, but he had no chance on the lines which he selected. He was boxing at a pace which he could never maintain, and without receiving any serious punishment save in the last few seconds he was a practically beaten man by the end of the third round. He had exhausted himself by his own efforts and could now only hope to win by getting home a knockout blow. I had him not only tired, but desperate as well, unable to follow any scheme of action save that which I selected. And it was only his great heart, splendid condition, and remarkable grit that carried him along into the sixth round, when the bout was stopped.

Since the event, several critics have seen fit to find fault with the match. They have asserted that Hayes was boxing right out of his class. Such however, is not the fact, for the seaman is a much better man than he has had the credit of being. He lost, and lost badly to me, for the simple reason that he had failed to form a plan of campaign which was adapted to the occasion. He just boxed as he wanted to box, only more so, without considering whether I was likely to fall in with his ideas. Had I gone in and mixed it, as another man might have been tempted to do, things might have panned out differently, just as I should, I hope, have adopted very different tactics, had Hayes elected to fight me in different fashion.

Chapter Three

Some of the Finer Points in the Game

The description of my tactics against Seaman Hayes may be taken as a guide to the most satisfactory method of meeting a rushing opponent. Not that Hayes is a rusher pure and simple, but rather that by boxing on the lines I did, I converted him into a fair imitation of the reckless charging fighter, who is always a dangerous opponent, but who is yet a man whom it is never difficult to beat, provided one keeps cool and steady and is fairly smart and quick on one's feet.

The rusher wants to get to close quarters, where he can pound away either at the face or body, and as he usually carries a kick in either hand and is moreover mainly regardless of any punishment which may be dealt out to him, it is usually advisable to baulk his intentions as far as possible. But when you see a contest in which one of these tearaway boxers is engaged, you will usually find that clinching forms its most striking feature. The rusher's opponent tries to meet his man with straight hitting; stands up to him, gets flurried and then goes into holds to avoid the other man's punches. Now, as rushing is scarcely likely to appeal to a man who is not possessed of a fair amount of physical strength, this is about the worst method which one could adopt against him.

For first of all these clinching intervals are just the very things he wants. They enable him to recover his wind, or rather to retain it, for if he has to keep rushing and swinging furiously, against a man who is able to neatly side-step him and to generally lead him a dance all over the ring, he will soon get blown. His pace will drop, and he will probably pull up for a breather. But this is just what you (supposing you to be opposed to a man of this character) are anxious above all, not to allow. The moment he pulls up, you ought to go right into him, administer a tap or so and then get away again. You will have annoyed him and he will probably forget his breathlessness, to come after you as furiously as before. Two or three rounds of this sort of thing ought to suffice to deliver him in a practically helpless condition into your hands.

Fighting in a Clinch

But another objection to the clinch is the difficulty of avoiding the temptation to push your opponent away. The referee is ordering you to break and your opponent is probably resting an his weight on you, with the result that you endeavour to push him back, in doing which you will only tire yourself and waste your strength.

There are times, of course, when clinching is fairly useful, and the tricks of fighting in clinches should certainly be studied. Firstly because every boxer of any ambition, will be sure, sooner or later to run up against an American boxer, even if he doesn't, as he probably will, take a trip across the Atlantic, and if he wants to be successful in his bouts with Americans, he win have to study up all he can about clinching and in-fighting, if he doesn't want to get badly left. For the American boxer makes in-fighting his speciality, and in the vast majority of cases is far more formidable at close quarters than he is at long range exchanges, Moreover the rules governing American fighting are far more elastic than those in use in this country, That "protect yourself at all times" clause permits, and indeed encourages, many things which a man would get disqualified for by an English referee, only that they are often done so skillfully as to defy detection.

Butting and the Use of the Head

Take for instance, the way in which American boxers and their imitators utilise their heads as weapons of offence. "Butting" is, of course, by no means unknown among British boxers, but it is rare to find any Briton using his head either so openly, or, on the other hand so secretly as do the men who have had an American apprenticeship.

I have boxed men in the States, who charged me with their heads down, and who would not have been even cautioned if they had rammed their crowns full into my face. Well, possibly they would have been, had they done so too frequently, but the average American referee is a fairly lenient man, usually willing to accept the explanation that trivial offences of this nature are purely accidental, if they do not occur too frequently. As can well be imagined the butting boxer is no very pleasant adversary. He may be met and damaged by well-applied uppercuts, but as he usually comes in and butts with judgment, this is not always easy of performance.

"Nudging" an opponent's chin in a clinch. My adversary is moving his head from side to side.

The most useful method, as I found in America, is to butt back. Fortunately, I have a pretty hard head and when an opponent had banged his skull against mine once or twice, he usually carne to the conclusion that the game wasn't as profitable or as pleasant as he had fancied it to be, and confined himself thenceforth to more legitimate methods of boxing.

But the above method of using the head is somewhat crude, and does not therefore appeal to the more polished exponents of the noble art. These men like to secure a similar advantage by subtler methods. They will come into a clinch, rest their heads on an opponent's chest just under his chin, while they jab at his ribs and stomach or pound his kidneys, but they have no idea of keeping their heads still in such circumstances. A head is a useful weapon in this position, which it would be a pity to neglect and so they shift it from side to side, or rather from shoulder to shoulder, administering a more or less vigorous tap each time they bring it past the other fellow's chin. After a fair amount of practice, they have discovered that they can produce almost the effect of a knockout punch without appearing either to have had the intention, or to have utilised the force necessary for such a feat.

It is, of course, very rare to see a man go down for the full count, from one of these insidious head nudges, but the thing has been known to happen even in England, one case, I believe, passing unnoticed by the judges at the last Army and Navy championships. Worked artistically, the serious nudge, designed to "out" or badly stagger a man, should always be accompanied by a punch whipped over for somewhere near the same spot, which blow will not only help in bringing about the desired effect, but will have the appearance of being the determining cause.

Please understand, that I neither advocate nor recommend this system of fighting. It is a style which should, I think, be sternly repressed, although it must be admitted that owing to the difficulty of detecting the practice, when it is skillfully carried out, it is to be feared that the desire for its suppression can remain little more than a pious one. These head nudges, you see, can easily happen quite accidentally in any clinch, so that it is difficult to do more than warn a man who is suspected of resorting to them. The only two men who can be absolutely certain that they are intentional are the guilty person and the victim, and though the latter may complain, a

Holding an opponent with your left and making it appear as though he were holding you.

referee will not always pay due attention, for the simple reason that it is by no means certain, that he may not be complaining without cause.

The really smart boxer, such a man for instance as ------, well, perhaps it is best not to mention names, will nudge, nudge; nudge, repeatedly, until his opponent gradually turns faint and giddy, and there is unfortunately, no counter to this form of attack. A man can, of course, if his conscience will allow him, mix in and return the compliment whenever he gets the chance. But this, at the best, is a most unsatisfactory state of affairs, and as a counsel of perfection, I would advise here as always, as strict an avoidance of clinches as one can contrive.

It is true that close in-fighting, body to body, with half-arm blows, hooks and jabs driven into the ribs and stomach are both useful and at times even pretty boxing, but nine out of every ten men who are addicted to this style of fighting, are always liable to contract the fault of holding and hitting, which cannot be too strongly deprecated.

Tricky Holds and
the Breakaway

Besides which, a scrupulously fair boxer is usually badly handicapped in a clinch. He may try to conform strictly to the rules, and may be opposed to a man who is up to every trick by which they can be evaded, with the possible result that when the referee utters a reprimand, he will address it to the innocent and unoffending party instead of the man who is actually guilty. One often sees a man cautioned for holding, when, as a matter of fact, he is really being held. In exasperation at this unmerited reproof, he will occasionally turn his heart to protest, when he will be made to pay the further penalty of receiving a punch in the face, from the delinquent, who has artfully released his hold, the moment the injured one's attention was distracted and proceeds to notify the fact by jabbing one of his fists home.

A very common method of employing this surreptitious hold is that of going into a clinch and slipping the left arm (let us say) under the other man's right, and then hooking the hand behind his back. Placed like this, the casual spectator, and even the experi-

A side step and legitimate kidney punch with
the knuckles of the glove.

enced one, can scarcely believe that the other fellow is not actually holding the imprisoned arm, this appearance being heightened by pressing the left arm upwards and thus tempting the other fellow to press with his right, for it is a peculiar fact that whenever you press against a man in any way, he will almost invariably press or push back. Worked like this, it wants a very clever observer indeed to detect which is really to blame. The actually innocent man looks as though he were holding his adversary's left arm, which, as a matter of fact, is really holding him, behind the back, and is always prepared to pull him forward on to a body punch whenever he tries to break loose. The holder pushes his elbow outwards now and again, and pretends to pull back, as though he were trying to get free, but was unable to do so, and every time that he makes this pretence he carefully tugs the other forward with his fingers and rams home an extra dig with his right. "Don't hold, Smith," yells the referee. Smith turns an exasperated eye on that official and starts to growl, "I am not holding," only to have the words pushed down his throat by Jones' fist. Another tug and he lurches forward, his chin possibly colliding with the top of Jones' head. The referee warns him again, and Jones' fist jabs into his stomach and ribs. His temper begins to vanish and with it his best chances of victory.

Now there is only one way of dealing with these tactics, but it is highly effective. They have to be endured for a time, because there is no profit in protesting. Wait for the moment when your opponent stiffens his arm and crooks his fingers for a tug. Then press your open glove against his elbow, press it against your side, and wrench yourself sharply away to the right. You may not fancy breaking away in this open fashion, for fear that when so doing, you will leave yourself open to a nasty hook or jab from his right to your face, but with ordinary care, you should be able to block this with your own left, while if you have executed the movement successfully you will have seriously damaged your opponent's left arm. Your wrench must be as sudden and forcible as you can make it, and if you are fortunate enough to be up against a man who makes a repeated use of the hold, you will before long have put his holding arm out of action. He will find himself quite unable to use it to any purpose, and will experience pain even when he puts it up in position.

One could fill pages with the various tricky holds which are

A foul kidney punch is delivered with
either the side or the heel of the glove.

practised by unscrupulous boxers, but space forbids my treating of more than one other, especially as the remainder are of comparative unimportance. The one referred to, however, is a very favourite trick with American pugilists, and is moreover a very difficult one to counter legitimately. It is used almost invariably as a follow to a missed lead for the face when the arm has gone past the head and rests on your shoulder. The pair of you go into a clinch and your opponent indulging in a hot spell of body punching with his right to the body, appears to be desirous of breaking away, but instead of so doing pulls your head down to meet a vicious jab. He may even repeat this once or twice, without attracting the notice of the referee at times, if the latter be, as he often is, unprepared to notice the manoeuvre and if the offender himself works in a sufficiently strenuous manner to disguise his action. There is no real counter to this move, save by adopting the illegitimate response of butting. One can, however, displace the arm from one's shoulder, by forcing the other man away, with your forearm under his chin, perhaps the best method of all, save that when one does this, one's body is exposed more than one cares about.

Kidney Punching

Every now and again the critics indulge freely in discussions as to whether the kidney punch should or should not be allowed. Those who would like to see it abolished, allege that it is a very dangerous blow, and it must be admitted that instances may be quoted of men who have had their kidneys severely punished with the result that their health has been seriously affected and their lives possibly shortened thereby. But even though this is a very strong argument for its abolition, there are so many reasons for its retention that one would not care to appeal for more than a rigid supervision of its delivery. There is one big merit in the kidney punch which well outweighs its disadvantages and that is that it is the best deterrent of persistent clinching in existence. A man who holds persistently and willfully almost always exposes his kidneys to punishment, and were the blow abolished it is to be feared that there would be even more clasping and clutching than there is at present.

But referees should be careful to note that the blow is only

Side-stepping a left lead from close quarters and going past your man.

dealt in a legitimate fashion, that is to say with the knuckles and not with the edge or heel of the hand. The latter form of striking this blow is not only illegal, but it is also far more dangerous and therefore more effective than the legitimate method, the mere act of delivering which naturally robs the punch of some part of its force.

Some boxers are much fonder of hammering away at the kidneys than others, but you will notice that the really experienced do not, as a rule, hammer persistently. They will deliver five or six blows and will then leave the spot severely alone for a round or so, after which they will resume their visitations and then give the kidney another rest.

There is, of course, a reason for this. The blows hurt and also heat the part affected, while the delay allows it to stiffen and thus become more susceptible to future punishment.

Here again, as with every other department of boxing, the good ring general will take a careful note of his rival's predilections. If an opponent is known to be fond of pounding the kidneys, it is not a bad plan to give him a chance to bring off his favourite blow, and then, just as he is about to deliver it, to draw back your arm quickly, so as to meet his descending forearm with your elbow. The contact is a somewhat painful one, and if one can only bring off the coup two or three times, the other fellow's fondness for the kidney blow will fade perceptibly.

How to Weaken an
Opponent's Arms

Though I have somewhat strongly deprecated the habit of clinching, it is as well to mention that it will nevertheless be frequently found to be a very useful move in the game. A clinch will often afford a boxer a much needed rest, besides which one can frequently sneak home a very useful punch, if one is fairly smart, on the break away. Then again, it is only in a clinch that one can tire and weaken a man's arms in a really satisfactory fashion. Say, that you have gone into one or that your opponent has come into one with you. Endeavour always on these occasions to get your arms above his. Then rest them just below his shoulders and press with all your force on his biceps and upper arms generally. Push them down and you will not only be safeguarding yourself against any punches, he may try to get home to your body, but will also be putting his arms out of action. For in addition to the weakening effect of your pressure, your opponent will be pressing back against you. He will endeavour, insensibly to thrust you away and will be thus further wearying his muscles. This, by the way, is a very favourite trick of Jack Johnson's and one which he employed with great effect against Tommy Burns.

The ex-champion, when he met the big Negro, undoubtedly played right into his opponent's hands by so persistently going into clinches with him, and as Johnson always rested all his weight on Tommy's upper arms, the Canadian soon lost the major portion of his hitting power. It is certain that Johnson would never have raised his hands in the air and allowed Burns to punch him in the ribs and stomach, had he not been satisfied that these blows would be much less forceful than usual. He took care to rob Tommy of the major portion of his strength, before he risked exposing his body, which he only did afterwards, partly out of a desire to play to the gallery and partly because he knew that by so doing, he would "get Tommy's goat" (help to make him lose his head).

But there are other ways and reasons for pressing an opponent's arms down. I have already mentioned that when you push or press a man, he will almost invariably push or press back. It is a little bit of human nature and a whole heap of ring craftiness is the result of a careful observation of this. Push against a man's forearm and he will push it back. Push both forearms down and you can slide your left off, whipping the right to his face. Both his arms will follow your right up and you can then dig your left to his unguarded stomach.

Getting Openings

Again, let us suppose that he comes at you with both hands raised to protect his face. His aim may be to get in close, so as to hammer at your body. You are, we will suppose, as smart and quick on your feet as you ought to be. Then, you will get away cleverly, just exactly the right distance and placing your left (let us say) on both his gloves, you will try to press these downwards. He will, almost certainly, push them upwards, and you can then whip your right in and under between his arms to his mouth or face.

As a general rule you will find, that as in more serious war, the interior lines are the best. By forcing your own gloves between your opponent's, you will be better able to strike an effective blow with either hand. At all times, or nearly always, endeavour to work your hands in between your adversary's. You can then either push these outwards and hit between; or, if he resents the pressure slip one or both hands out, and whipping round his guard, hook him in the face.

When you are up against an opponent who keeps his guard high and refuses to give you a chance at his face, it is the best plan to feint openly for the stomach, with your other hand raised, apparently solely for the purpose of protecting your own features. His hands will then come down to form a barrier for his stomach, and you will have a chance of driving your other fist where you wish to send it, namely, to the nose, eyes, or mouth.

The Neck a Good Mark

In my opinion, I do not think that the average boxer pays half enough attention to the nape of the neck, as a target for attack. A good punch properly sent to that spot will be found to be very effective, and yet the vast majority of pugilists confine their attacks to that region, to dropping deliveries hooked there during a clinch. But a far more useful punch than any of these can be got home in the following manner. A man comes at you with a rush, when if you side step him neatly, turning swiftly as he goes past, you can then drive home a straight heavy punch with the knuckles full in the nape of the neck. If you get home well, you can at times knock a man out with this blow. I have done so on numerous occasions, the last one being when I knocked out Spike Robson, with this delivery in our championship battle at the National Sporting Club. In this connection I may mention that I have heard it stated that the nape of the neck is one of the vital spots in Jiu-Jitsu, and that Japanese experts at that form of physical combat have been known to even kill an opponent with this delivery, although, of course, in their case it possesses its deadly character, simply and solely when it is dealt with the edge of the naked hand.

In spite of this, however, it should be remembered that the neck is a very sensitive part of the human anatomy, and that punches

Having passed him, turn swiftly and send a punch straight for the nape of the neck.

received there can be felt for days afterwards.

Talking in the Ring

Many famous boxers set great store on the use of their tongues while engaged in a contest. They talk "at" their opponents, gibe and chaff them and seek by this means, as by every other they can contrive to disturb their adversary's equanimity. Freddie Welsh, I believe, depressed Johnny Summers considerably by asking him where he had left his punch and by promising to speak highly of the game mariner in which he was taking his gruel. The trick may be a useful one in certain cases, as it may either depress or annoy your adversary, but personally I do not set any great store by it. On the contrary, I have been very glad on at least one occasion that my opponent was so fond of talking at me. Here again I refer to the Spike Robson contest. Spike had closed up my right eye, and had damaged it so much that the sight of the left was also affected. Indeed, I could not at times locate him at all by the sense of sight, and was indebted to his tongue for discovering his precise position. For fully four or five rounds, he was merely a shadowy flitting shape, and it was only by the constant stream of chaff which he was employing that I was able to keep myself prepared for the direction from which an attack was likely to arrive, or to make an attempt at punching him with any real hope of success.

It is, of course, quite probable that a boxer will find a ready flow of sarcasm and innuendo a most useful weapon in the ring, but this weapon, like all the others, should always be used with discretion.

Side-Stepping and Ducking

I suppose that every boxer is aware that the skillful use of the feet and head are far more important as defensive moves than any block or parry which can be made with the arms. A good guard is undoubtedly a good asset, but there are quite three or four reasons why a man should prefer avoiding, to either stopping or parrying a blow.

For one reason, repeated stopping must inevitably mean bruises and weariness. A jarred nerve, from the impact of a heavy blow, may easily paralyse or partially paralyse the guarding arm, if

The punch to the nape of the neck (often a knockout punch)
may be sent home against a man who rushes with
his head down, following a side-step.

only for the period of a few seconds, during which time the limb in question will be practically useless either for defensive or offensive purposes, while its subsequent utility will almost certainly be considerably impaired.

In addition to this, a guard, parry, or block, however skillfully and certainly it may be employed, is always a waste of time, as well as of energy. If one side steps or ducks a blow, one has always both hands at liberty with which to retaliate, and, better still, one has thrown one's opponent off his balance, bringing him right in to receive a punch; instead of forcing him to recoil, or being forced to recoil oneself, out of distance.

But, as already stated, it is to be supposed that every boxer is well acquainted with these reasons for the value of the side-step or duck. It gets impressed on one in every boxing school, and is one of the numerous items which go to make up the curriculum of boxing. But this instruction often stops short at the mere act of side-stepping or ducking, without any further hints being imparted as to when, where, or how to employ these methods of avoiding to the best advantage.

A man learns how to be quick on his feet and how to dodge cleverly, with the result that he makes a point of always slipping away either in haphazard fashion or else to one particular side. The latter is actually a very usual habit with many boxers, far more usual, indeed, than might be ordinarily supposed, and, consequently, a full appreciation of this fact will be of the greatest advantage to the boxer who uses his powers of observation.

Say that you are up against a man who is doing his best to force the exchanges, but who, at the same time, betrays the fact that he is watching your every move. Side-step all his attacks to the right, until he gets it fixed in his mind that this is a regular habit of yours. Then watch his eye, and as soon as you see that he has got firm hold of that idea, watch for his next rush and then go away to the left. He will come quickly at you, swerving so as to defeat your old right side slip, and missing you will probably go stumbling ahead, very much at your mercy.

This is a hint with, of course, numerous applications. You must beware of being similarly caught yourself, and may also look out for opportunities of catching the man with the pet side step: Just as you may also watch carefully for the man with the regular duck.

Side-Stepping and ducking a right swing and
driving the right to the body.

You may feint to make him duck and then upper cut or jab him as he does so, or you may coax another man to follow out this policy and cause him to fall forward against you as he strives to get home an effective blow.

The Best Dodge

Most boxers make the mistake of overdoing this side-stepping business, however. It pleases them immensely to make their opponents miss them by feet or yards, quite forgetting that when so doing they go out of distance themselves and are unable to take advantage of their adversary's loss of balance. It is, therefore, far wiser to cultivate a swift body swerve or twist, usually from the hips, which will just take one out of range and yet enable one to return within striking distance immediately. Packey McFarland is very smart at this move, and his methods are well worth studying on this account alone. The whole secret, of course, lies in an absolutely accurate judgment of both time and distance. For it must be remembered that a man when hitting directs all his force to getting home at one exact spot, and that if his target be removed even a couple of inches, his blow will be deprived of its force quite as fully as if he were a couple of yards away.

Blocking and Guarding

In a treatise on Ringcraft, there should be no place for any instruction as to guarding or parrying a blow, that being a department of boxing itself, but it may be as well to mention that there' are more ways of stopping a blow than that of interposing an arm or glove between it and its objective. There is the method of "checking" or breaking the force of the delivery, by giving a more or less powerful tap or push against the upper arm or shoulder of the arm delivering the punch, This method serves a double purpose, by the way, inasmuch as it not only breaks the force of the blow even when it does not stop the punch altogether, but also proves very tiring to the man against whom it is utilised. It tires his hitting muscles to a really remarkable extent, and may deprive him of his speed in parrying as well as hitting. But it depends mainly for its success on the possession of one, or rather two qualities; a long reach and great rapidity of movement. A boxer who "blocks" in this fashion has to push his arm the full length of his opponent's, and has also to push it to its target, before that opponent's punch can have travelled any great distance, despite the fact that the push must start after the punch has got off on its journey. A short-reached man may use the "block," perhaps, and use it successfully, but he will have to be very quick indeed to be able to do so.

Another method of parrying, and one which is a great favourite with American boxers, can also only be relied on at all satisfactorily by a man who is very quick with his arms. It means, moreover, taking the outside position, and to a certain extent allowing one's opponent to work his arms inside yours. I have deprecated doing anything of the kind already, and so would therefore wish, if possible, to explain the difference between the real exterior (and, therefore, wrong) position and the apparent exterior one in this instance.

The one we are dealing with, which consists of knocking a man's punch inwards, is not an actual surrender of the interior lines, but rather an apparent offering of them to one's opponent. The advantage of it lies in the fact that practically every punch slants more or less inwards. The hook or swing, of course, does so excessively, but even the straight blow slants in a little from the shoulder to the spot at which it is aimed.

Consequently, it requires no vast amount calculation to realise that it is far easier to knock a blow inwards, helping it along the road it is already travelling, than it is to knock it outwards, *against* the force which is driving it. A smart tap, applied against the forearm or wrist just before the blow would arrive at its destination, will, therefore, not only deflect the blow itself, without the cost of any great exertion, but will partially turn the striker round and thereby expose him to attack. This is a very useful style of parrying, but it naturally demands plenty of both speed and accuracy to be successful.

As a final word of advice on defensive tactics in general, I would always strongly recommend the careful cultivation of one and all, and a carefully studied variation in their use.

Make yourself sound first in the simpler methods, and then proceed carefully with the more advanced ones. Practise, practise, practise, and neglect no possible opportunity for study. Remember, above everything, that when you cease to improve, the hour of retrogression has struck.

On Putting a Man Out

Everyone, of course, knows the knockout punches. There are plenty of them; far more than most people suspect. Almost any blow may be the "sleep-producer," provided it only lands heavily enough. I have seen men put down and out with a kidney blow, when they have been in pretty bad condition, and have, as already stated, not infrequently put opponents "out" with a blow on the neck.

There is no necessity here to go exhaustively into the subject of how to send a man down for the full count, but it may be as well to devote a few lines to some hints as to the best method of finishing a man who is reeling on his feet and who is in a more or less groggy condition. You will often see a boxer staggering about the ring, wobbling at the knees and with both gloves covering his face, while his opponent is wasting his energy in wild attempts to hook him on his well-protected jaw. The groggy one reels into his opponent; falls down, perhaps, but rises again, and eventually manages to last out the round, only to turn the tables in the next, perhaps.

There is one golden rule for a situation like this. The staggering man may be really in a bad way, or may be only feigning to be so, in the hope of trapping his antagonist into a wild swing or hook which will leave him open. In either situation, it is as well to safeguard oneself against accidents, and in both it is practically invariably the case, that the "groggy one" leaves his stomach absolutely unprotected. Work in to him, therefore, and push one of your gloves or forearms against his gloves, partly so as to straighten him up and partly to keep them from moving, and then drive for his stomach for all you are worth with the other hand. The placing of your hands should, of course, be simultaneous, in order first that your move may not be suspected, and secondly, that the idea should be conveyed that your real attack is at the face. The body blow will make him double up, a second may bring him down for good, even if the first hasn't, while, if neither desirable event occurs, the covering gloves will almost inevitably be withdrawn, thereby exposing the jaw to a finishing punch.

Stopping an opponent who comes in covered up and holding left ready for swinging uppercut for body or swing or hook for jaw.

Slacking Off

I think I have already laid sufficient stress on the fact that a boxer can never afford to ease up during the course of a round. He should always keep hard at work from gong to gong, and never allow his opponent even the briefest of rests. He should always endeavour to enter the ring in such a sound condition that he can box in this strenuous fashion, without unduly distressing himself in any way. Drive at your man all the time, as hard and as fast as you can, try and make him get out of his stride and keep him out of his stride, when you will have him panting almost before he knows where he is. No matter how the pace is telling on you, do not allow him to rest and never think of resting yourself until the gong signals that you may do so. Rest then and rest immediately. The moment the bell has gone, let all your muscles go loose and slouch to your corner as easily as you can. It does not matter in the least if your opponent and the spectators think that you are all in. You are boxing to win, not to avoid giving people erroneous ideas about your condition. It may, indeed, help you considerably, if your opponent does fancy that he has you well beaten. For he may then come at you harder than ever in the next round and thereby exhaust himself still more.

But your main idea in going limp like this is really that you may get as much rest during the minute interval as you can. A quick sprightly run to your corner may look very pretty as a spectacle, and may evoke a certain amount of admiration, but it is useless for any other purpose and therefore unnecessary. Other things being equal, it is an excellent plan to endeavour to so arrange matters that the round terminates in close proximity to your own corner, as you will then have only a few paces to go before sinking into your chair, while your opponent will be put to the exertion of crossing the ring to his own. This is a little thing and scarcely worth troubling about, it may be thought, but you will find that these little things count in a 20 round contest.

Should the round, however, terminate at any distance from your corner, try and arrange it so that it does so near the ropes, and then do not hesitate to clutch this to help you as you stroll back. Tell your seconds to meet you as you come back and to support you during the last yard or so, and, by the way, it is usually a good plan to get one of them to hold a watch, so that he may signal you when you are entering on the last half-minute.

The Thirty Seconds Spurt

It is an excellent plan to put on a spurt during this period, because you will usually find that a referee is more impressed by what happens during the last thirty seconds of a round than he often is by the doings of any previous sixty. For one thing, that last minute is fresher in the memory, and for another, the well trained man, who has sedulously forced the pace, or rather lured his opponent into doing so from the gong, should be in far better condition during this final stage of the round. His opponent will be somewhat blown and, therefore, almost at his mercy. So that if a man has boxed smartly and cleverly on the lines laid down in the last chapter, he should have very few points against him, despite the fact that he has been more or less on the defence, or at all events, getting away; and certainly no more points than he can wipe out in a whirlwind finish.

After a few rounds, the other fellow will probably spot the game, and will, if he is at all experienced, come to some similar arrangement with his seconds; but the success of his attempts at boxing in this fashion will depend on the way in which he is forced to fight at the commencement of each round, and on the relative condition of the two men, a factor which yields yet one more proof that boxing contests can be most surely gained in one's training quarters, and that speed and stamina are every whit as, if not even more important than, skill and hitting power.

How to Take the Count

There is one other instance in which a man is justified in taking a rest, and that is when he is sent to the boards by a punch. The other fellow is also resting, but then you are in greater need of rest than he is at the moment. Never allow any false pride to influence you at this point. If you have been sent down, you will probably be feeling a bit shaken, and since the rule allows you ten seconds in which to regain your feet, it is only an absurd vanity which can argue that you should not fully enjoy that interval. You can do no good by leaping to your feet earlier, for in any circumstances, the rest will be an all too brief one. You have been shaken and have also been exposed in a position of inferiority, a position which you can only straighten out by returning to your work in a thoroughly cool and collected fashion. Do not therefore, lie asprawl on the boards, however that position may appeal to you. Get to your knees, or rather to one knee, with your other foot firmly placed, as quickly as you possibly can, and remain there, with all your muscles loose until nine seconds have been counted out. Rise promptly then and be as careful and prudent as you can. Your opponent will very possibly rush up at once, eager to finish you off, before you can recover your full powers, and if you have been really badly shaken, your quick footwork will be your only salvation, while should you have only gone down to a more or less ineffective punch and be thus able to rise in full possession of your faculties, you may be able to meet his rush with a heavy delivery, which may perhaps turn the tables completely.

Preliminary Ringcraft

There are some boxers, mostly Americans, who spare no pains in this department, which has for its aim, the demoralisation of an opponent, prior to the opening of the contest. They will despatch emissaries to their opponent's training quarters, who will try to depress the poor fellow's spirits, by weird tales of their man's terrible deeds, it being, of course, understood that these emissaries always profess a fervent desire for the nervous one's success. They don't like "the terror" and want badly to see him beaten, but the man capable of achieving that feat must beware of this and look out for that; must remember what happened to so-and-so; while it is really surprising that he has never heard of "the terror's" diabolical cleverness in this direction.

This is the first act, with another to be played as soon as the men get in the ring. For when they arrive there, the wily craftsman will stroll round, cool and superbly calm, with an air of the most confident superiority, while he objects to his opponent's bandages, criticises the general arrangements, and generally appears to be dissatisfied with the prospects of there being a slight delay before the slaughter commences.

This is the personal equation, which must always be reckoned with. It may sound rather unimportant, but I have often known it to be the determining factor in a contest.

By the way, talking of bandages, I can remember one little piece of preliminary ring craftiness which had a most important effect on the career of a boxer of worldwide reputation. But as he had won his fame abroad, his abilities were somewhat doubted in his own district and it was decided to give him a very severe trial before accepting the estimation which others had formed of him, as being an absolutely correct one.

A very stiff opponent was selected, a much older, heavier boxer, who had had years of experience and who, had he been at all willing to take care of himself, might have found a place among the world's champions. Our hero realised that he was taking on a very formidable task and felt that he would need every assistance, artificial or otherwise, if he was to prove successful.

Now, there is a brand of bandage used in America and occasionally in this country, which, while fairly innocent in appearance, has the quality of hardening into a substance which strongly resembles marble, as soon as the hands commence to perspire. It was felt that the experienced pugilist would know all about these bandages, and would consequently strongly object to their use, so it was resolved to trick him if possible, and having pondered over the subject, the following ruse was put into operation.

An ordinary simple and perfectly innocent bandage was put on the left hand, while the objectionable one was strapped round the right knuckles. The two men then entered the ring and submitted their hands for each other's inspection. The old hand at once objected to the bandage on his opponent's right, and after due protest and argument the other retired to change it, returning to the ring with his left hand gloved and the right bandaged in a perfectly unobjectionable manner. The left hand had, of course, been previously examined and it never occurred to anyone to ask for a second inspection.

The bout commenced and the first time that left found the eye, it opened a nasty gash. This worried the old boy, who found that left continually pecking away at his face and working sad havoc with each visit. He lost blood freely and finally collapsed before the bout had run its course, while the new star's reputation as a formidable puncher went up several places.

Straight Hitting Versus Swings

The round arm boxer has gained a lot of fame of late years, and there are plenty of critics who will tell you that the old upright,

straight style of boxing which used to be the fashion has now become exploded. But it only needs practice to convince anyone that the straight blow will always get there before the swing or the hook. Both the others, but especially the last, are frequently useful, but they can never compare with the straight punch for either force, speed, or effect. Besides which the man who hits straight has little need to worry about his hands. His blows land squarely with the force of the impact well distributed, while the blows of the swinger land anyhow and he is always liable to the danger of suffering from a dislocated thumb or knuckles. But these remarks belong to a treatise on boxing, and have little to do with Ringcraft.

Addendum

Jim Driscoll's
Final Fight

DISCOLL BEATEN

Ledoux Wins In The 10th Round

TRIUMPH OF YOUTH

The Times of London
October 21, 1919

Charles Ledoux (France) beat Jim Driscoll (Wales) in the 16th round of a 20-round contest at the National Sporting Club, Covent Garden, last night. Driscoll's seconds threw up the sponge.

The interest of many who attended the fight was blended with regret that Driscoll should, in his 39th year, have been persuaded to pit himself against so formidable an opponent as Charles Ledoux. The latter started with an advantage of nearly 12 years in age; he has beaten many of our best men in his own class in a decisive way - such men as Johnny Hughes, Curley Walker, Bill Beynon, and Digger Stanley. Ledoux won the Bantamweight Championship of the world by his defeat of the letter in 1912, but he has now grown out of that class, and the fight last night was at 8st. 11lb.

Driscoll was universally acknowledged the featherweight champion of the world after his defeat of Abe Attell in 1909; he retired undefeated in 1913 - to make his present attempt to "come back" earlier in this year. His last appearance at the National Sporting Club was on January 27, 1913, when he met and drew with Owen Moran. A few months ago Driscoll drew with Francis Rossi, but the rounds on that occasion were only of two minutes' duration.

The Fight

The fight started quickly, both men sparring for an opening, but even at this early stage the contrast between the styles of the two men was very marked. Driscoll stood up and principally relied upon his straight left, while the Frenchman adopted a crouching attitude and tried to rush in, swinging either hand alternately. Driscoll had little difficulty in evading Ledoux's rushes, and boxed coolly and with a much more apparent ease. In the second round Ledoux tried again to rush in, but Driscoll waited quietly and always had a stinging left-hander to bring him up short, or merely side-stepped his opponent and drove his right to Ledoux's ear or face.

In the third round Driscoll smiled; he was completely outboxing his man, and reached his opponent's face with either hand quite easily. It was noticeable in this and the succeeding rounds that when it came to in-fighting Driscoll always secured the inner berth. Driscoll seemed a little shaken once or twice by the Frenchman's rushes, but he was always quite ready to "mix matters". In the fifth round Driscoll used his superior height to the greatest advantage; he was doing all the leading, and piling up a tremendous score in points. There was far more variety in his punches, and he seldom lost a chance of reaching his opponent's face or body. It was noticeable how cleverly Driscoll used the ring for his own advantage; he rarely shifted his ground, but kept Ledoux moving all the time and continually caught him in a corner.

The next two rounds were very similar to the preceding ones, there was one man in the ring so far as the scoring was concerned. The eighth round was a magnificent one, and was the most stirring of any up to this point. Early in the round a right-handed swing made Driscoll's mouth bleed. The Welshman replied with a stinging uppercut to the nose that shook Ledoux severely and drew blood. This was followed by a heavy left-hander on the Frenchman's left eye, which at once swelled up.

In the ninth round Driscoll was all over his man, time after time reaching the damaged eye and driving right and left to jaw and face repeatedly. Ledoux had a bad time and was well within himself all the time. In the 10th round Ledoux did better, but all his blows glanced off the side of face or chin, owing to Driscoll's perfect dodging and ducking. Although Ledoux did the leading, it was Driscoll who scored the points again, and he never lost a chance of jabbing his opponent's eye, which was still swelling more and more.

Jim Driscoll (right) versus Charles Ledoux in Driscoll's final fight.

In the 11th round Ledoux seemed to be weakening, and it looked as though Driscoll might knock him out. The older man seemed as strong as ever and made his opponent look like a novice. Ledoux took things quietly in the next round and was content to cover up and rest. Even so, Driscoll managed to pierce his defence and score.

Driscoll, for his part, had been waiting during the 13th round for an opportunity to reach his opponent's chin with an uppercut. He seemed, however, to be weakening, but quite possibly this was for Ledoux's benefit. Driscoll stated scoring a great ratio in the next round using his right, of which little had been seen up to this point. Ledoux's defense seemed to be weakening, and he took a good deal of punishment.

A dramatic change came over the fight in the 15th round. A heavy right-handed punch on Driscoll's jaw shook him badly. For the rest of the round he was almost defenceless, although, even when desperately weak, his cleverness in covering up and dodging was wonderful. By the end of the round he was tottering, and only the bell saved him from being knocked out. At the beginning of the next and last round it was apparent that Driscoll could hardly stand. He staggered towards the centre of the ring, but his seconds at once gave in for him.

It was a memorable fight, which no one who saw could ever forget. Driscoll was seen at his best, and although beaten in the end by his opponent's youth and strength, he can retire with little, if any, loss of his prestige. The loser received a tremendous ovation at the end, which he fully deserved.

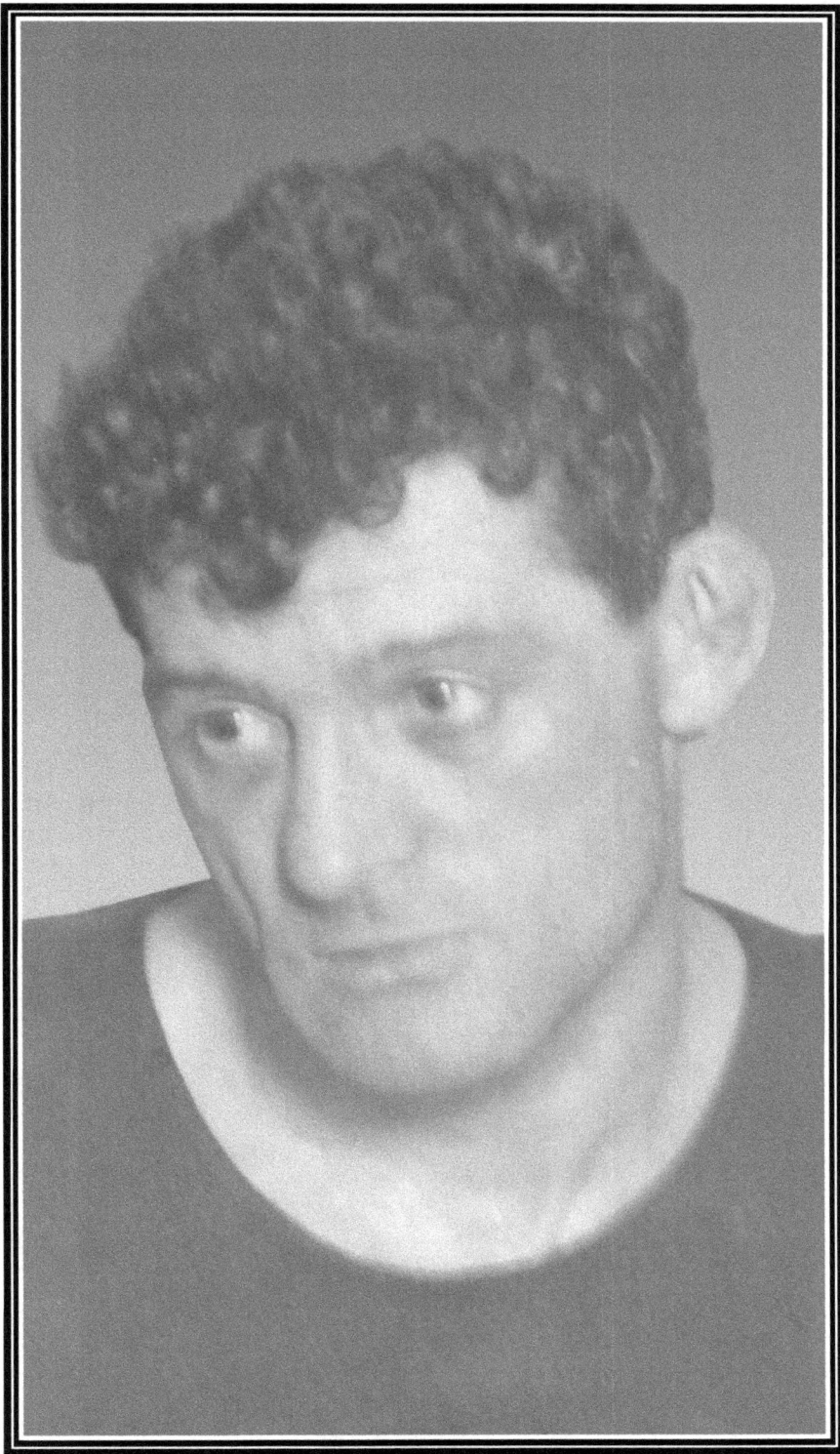

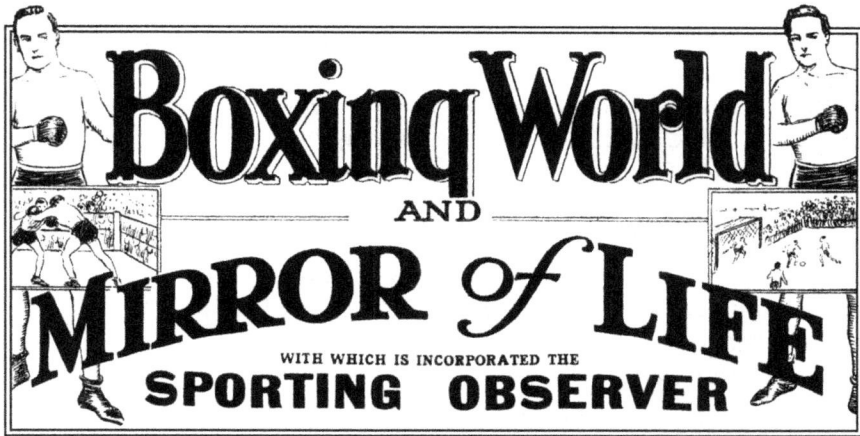

Boxing World

AND

MIRROR of LIFE

WITH WHICH IS INCORPORATED THE

SPORTING OBSERVER

VOL. XLVIII., NO. 1350. (Entered at Stationers' Hall.)   LONDON : SAT., NOV. 1ST, 1919.   **2d.**

The Defeat of Peerless Jim Driscoll

His Brilliant Boxing with Ledoux

By J. Frank Bradley

I am very sorry I have lived to see Jim Driscoll beaten!

Far be it from me to try to deprive Charles Ledoux of one iota of the credit he has gained for being the first to defeat the incomparable, the peerless Jim Driscoll, but we all know, and even Ledoux and his best friends will admit that he could never have beaten Driscoll had the latter been at anything like his best. And I will go further and say that had Driscoll possessed two good hands he would have beaten Ledoux last week.

Many people say and believe that it was Driscoll's age that beat him, and on the day after the contest, when the friends of both men met at the Club, Mons. Descamps, the manager of Ledoux, Carpentier and others, said that although Ledoux won on the previous night, it was not he but thirty-nine years that beat Driscoll. To this I do not subscribe. I had a letter from Mr. Joe Summerhayes, a close friend of Driscoll's, a couple of weeks before the contest, and he told me that Driscoll hat severely hurt his hand in a motor mishap. Mr. Summerhayes was running a boxing show at Wellington, near Taunton, Somerset, and Driscoll went there to box exhibition as thee show was for the Blind Soldiers' Institute, and Jim was ever ready and willing to give his services in the cause of sweet charity. There was a motor accident and Jim and Mr. Summerhayes were in it. This is what the latter gentleman wrote to me in a letter dated October 5th:

> "Of course you know that Jim hurt his thumb at Taunton, and after that we got stuck up ten miles from anywhere, in the middle of the night, in a motor smash, and I thought it was all over with two of your Cardiff pals, Jim and your humble."

In a later letter Mr. Summerhayes wrote:

> "I am glad to say that Jim is boxing fine. I have just come from his quarters … but his thumb is still weak."

A few days before the contest, Driscoll wrote to me, and in his letter he said:

> "I jumped my thumb, but expect it will be all right by Tuesday or Wednesday."

Now I may be accused of having a partiality for Driscoll, and I candidly admit that I have, and always have had, ever since I saw him box the first time. But I ask them who know him, in and out of the ring, in public as well as in private life, have I not every cause and reason to respect and admire Jim Driscoll? I have written much about Driscoll in past years, and always in his favour. I could not do otherwise! And I am writing these lines with a very heavy heart, but I am saying the truth, and what I think, and honestly believe. I can say with Pope:

> "Who dares think one thing and another tell,
> My heart detests his as the gates of hell."

I have been amongst boxers and boxing for more than 45 years and have met the best men the modern boxing world has produced, both in America and England. I have never met a man, a boxer, whom I admired and respected, both in and out of the ring, as I admire and respect Jim Driscoll! I have never seen his equal in the ring, as a boxer, for perfect science, ease, elegance, judgment and all else that goes to form the true English style of boxing. Out of the ring I have never met a straighter, more honest, more straightforward or better man - gentleman and sportsman (synonymous terms!) than Jim Driscoll, and now, in his hour of defeat, I know his friends will be brought closer to him and will show their appreciation of his sterling qualities by tangible and liberal proofs. When I was in Jim's dressing room with Mr. Norman Clark, after the contest, Mr. W. Mortimer, the backer of Johnny Basham, said he would back Driscoll against Ledoux or anybody else at 9st. for £2,000 or anything less, the contest to be of fifteen rounds, He also said that all sportsmen should subscribe for a testimonial for Driscoll, and he was prepared to open it by giving £100. Another gentleman at once promised £100, and a third gentleman said he would give £50. Mr. Summerhayes has forwarded a cheque for £100 to Mr. Bettinson for the "Driscoll Testimonial Fund", and, no doubt, this same fund will speedily assume colossal proportions. And Jim deserves it - every penny of it - however much it may total!

And now I must say something about the contest. Driscoll dropped into his orthodox, elegant, upright position, whilst Ledoux crouched somewhat, and this cause Driscoll's advantage in height to seem more pronounced. Ledoux was the first to begin and he let go at Jim's head with his left, but Driscoll very easily avoided the blow by a slight backward movement of his head. Ledoux tried again, but missed once more. It was now clear to the veriest novice that Driscoll was the master as far as boxing was concerned. He shot his left out straight as an arrow, and found the Frenchman "at home".

And by degrees, as they began to warm to their work and their eyes found their distance, the boxing became faster. Jim's left kept shooting out into the face of the Frenchman, as straight as a gun barrel, and he never missed one single stroke. But I noticed that his good left hand seemed to have lost its sting. It has lost none of its speed, and that means power, and Jim was judging his distances to the sixtieth part of an inch, and still the Frenchman's head never flew back, as I have those of some of Driscoll's opponents do, and I at once guessed that his left hand had "gone back" on him. He kept after his opponent, which was splendid generalship, as it prevented Ledoux from attacking, and Jim knew that with his damaged "fin" he would not be able to keep the strong Frenchman at a safe distance. Driscoll's work was beautiful, and he had a man in front of him who was able to show off his superb skill to the greatest advantage. Driscoll boxed like the master he is and gave Ledoux an excellent lesson in the Noble Art. It was a case of professor and pupil, and Driscoll's masterly avoidance, guarding or stopping of Ledoux's blows brought forth frequent and hearty applause from the spectators.

Those of my readers who have seen Driscoll in contests seven to eight years ago - with Robson, Hayes, Poesy and others, will no doubt remember that when he got home on his opponent's face with his perfect straight left blows, the recipient's head flew back almost between his shoulders, and a few such rasping blows quickly reduced the man's strength and made an opening in Driscoll's right. But when he hit Ledoux the Frenchman's head did not fly back as of old, and this proved to me that Jim's best weapon had failed him. If Driscoll's had had been thoroughly sound he would have quickly reduced Ledoux's strength, but we know that when the thumb is injured and weak we cannot close the first tightly, and when a "loose hand" comes into contact with an opponent's face, the impact drives the loosely-held fingers inward and make the hand a sort of buffer, the "give" of the fingers effectually robbing the blow of its force. Again, the straight left is used primarily to confuse or weaken a man, and secondly to make an opening for the right. Driscoll's weak hand entirely prevented him from making an opening for the right, and he was obliged to "chance it" when there was no opening. To get his right in at all - his only chance - he was obliged to use the right in a downward chop, like a reversed upper-cut, as Ledoux's shoulder partly covered his jaw, and as soon as he saw Driscoll's right hand move in his direction, a quick downward turn of his head took the "point" out of the reach of the coming hand and left nothing but the side and back of the head for Driscoll to hit. Had Jim possessed a sound left, he would never have let his right go until he had made an opening, but, being quite

AN IMPRESSION OF LEDOUX TRYING TO GET PAST DRISCOLL'S LEFT

AND WHENEVER HE SUCCEEDED JIMMY WAS NOT "AT HOME"

DURING THE IN-FIGHTING LEDOUX' KIDNEYS MUST HAVE FELT THAT THERE WAS AN AERIAL BOMB-ARDMENT GOING ON

AFTER 15 ROUNDS OF INVALUABLE INSTRUCTION IN THE ART OF BOXING LEDOUX MUST HAVE FELT LIKE DOING THIS.

LUCK FAVOURED LEDOUX IN THE 15TH RO. AND A LUCKY THING FOR HIM IT DID

M. DESCAMPS GIVES A FEW TIPS AT THE END OF THE FIRST ROUND

GOD OF YOUTH

BUT THIS IS THE LITTLE GENTLEMAN WHO WAS SOLELY RESPONSIBLE FOR LEDOUX' LUCKY VICTORY

AND A FEW MORE AT THE END OF THE FOURTEENTH

Our artist's impressions of the Ledoux-Driscoll contest.

unable to make such an opening, he "chanced the right" often enough, in the hopes of getting one home that would, at least, daze the Frenchman and make an opening for a straight right-hander that would have finished the job.

Jim tried hard to feint and fiddle his man into leaving an opening, but without a punishing left - or with a crippled left - (a distinction without a difference) it is impossible to make such an opening, If it had been possible, Jim would have done it, and because he did not I am convinced that he could not, and if he couldn't then nobody else can, and, therefore, it is logically impossible. Jim tired himself by his exertions, and his left being all but useless made him work much harder, as he could not hit defensively to keep Ledoux out - and the left hand is the chief item in defensive hitting - and so when Ledoux, with strength unimpaired by the uselessness of Driscoll's sinister hand, went in furiously to attack Driscoll could only defend himself by avoidance - head and footwork - and not, as he would have done, by defensive hitting - punishing and weakening his opponent and at the same time foiling his attack. Ledoux kept up a fierce attack in the fifteenth round, and got in some blows on Jim's head and body that he would never have succeeded in landing if Driscoll had possessed a sound left hand - and then the end came! Driscoll reeled to his corner when the gong sounded the end of the round, and when the beginning of round sixteen was signalled, his seconds saw, as he kept his seat, that he was unable to continue, and, much against the wish of the plucky Driscoll, threw a towel into the ring in a token of defeat.

Again I say, in spite of what many people say and what many sporting scribes have written, that is was NOT Driscoll's years, but his crippled left hand that beat the most brilliant boxer I have ever seen or ever shall see.

I went to Jim's dressing room after the contest, and there was a most uncomfortable lump in my throat as I shook hands with him. I could not speak, but Jim knew my feelings.

"Look here, Frank," he said, as he drew forth his hand from the folds of his dressing gown, or blanket, for my inspection. "I couldn't keep him out with that, could I?" and I sadly shook my head.

Mr. Norman Clark was with me, and he said to me, "We've seen the cleverest boxer we shall ever see beaten by a man who would not have stood ten rounds before him if he had had two good hands," and I agreed with him.

I don't know exactly what will be done in the matter of the testimonial, but I know every sportsman in Great Britain will give what he can afford - many will give more than they can afford, and I think I shall be one of them.

In future years the name of Jim Driscoll will be spoken with respect by future generations, and as we read and speak of such brilliant fighters and good men as Jack Boughton, Tom Johnson, John Jackson, Jem Belcher, John Gully, Tom Cribb, Tom Spring, Jem Ward, Jack Randall, Dick Curtis and others of the old Prize Ring, so will Jim Driscoll's name be uttered with respect and admiration as the most brilliant boxer of the gloving era.

Driscoll had lived and fought for the public, and I am sure that they will see to it that he, a soldier, a boxer, and, above all, a gentleman and a sportsman, will receive an adequate reward for all he has done, not only for the boxing game, but also for charity. Hood wrote:

> "Alas for the rarity
> Of Christian Charity
> Under the sun!"

And Driscoll's charitable acts have rarely been equalled. Who does not remember how he cancelled lucrative engagements in America to come over and box for the Nazareth House? An institution for which he has been the means of securing thousands of pounds.

His defeat is owing, in a great measure, to his efforts on behalf of a charitable institution, the Blind Soldiers' Institute, and it was whilst sparring here for Sweet Charity's sake that he received the injury which brought about his defeat. It is fitting that this should be so, and as a gentleman said in a letter just received by me:

> "Jim has given his whole life, and now his championship,
> to charity, and I hope he will not be forgotten in his pres-
> ent trial and in his future."

Every boxer ought to take Jim Driscoll as his model - both in and out of the ring. Their thanks are due to him and his clean actions, for their being allowed to box and gain a living today by that means. He is a model for every boxer when in the ring, as well as for every young man when out of the ring. But I need not try to tell people of Driscoll's greatness or his goodness. Everybody knows about them, and I am only wasting time and space in reminding people of them.

> "To gild refined gold, to paint the lilly,
> To throw a perfume on the violet,
> Is wasteful and ridiculous excess."

And to refer to Driscoll's greatness as a boxer and his goodness, generosity and straightforwardness as a man is an equally "wasteful and ridiculous excess."

FISTIC COMMENTS: THE DRISCOLL TESTIMONIAL

By the *Boxing World and Mirror of Life* Editorial Board

Although Jim Driscoll has said he is ready to again try to overcome Charles Ledoux, it is to be hoped that his friends will be able to persuade him to refrain from taking another chance. That he should want to after having given the Frenchman such a lesson in boxing before Nature had her say is not surprising, and any would be a bold man that would say defeat would be Driscoll's portion again, but for the reason that it might a second match should not be mooted.

When it was first suggested that Driscoll and Ledoux should meet, I expressed the opinion that Jim should have nothing to do with the Frenchman, and although I would have been sorry to have missed the great display of boxing Driscoll gave, I wish he had adhered to a decision he arrived at close upon seven years ago after his drawn battle with Owen Moran at the National Sporting Club, where he was never beaten until last week.

In contributing a couple of columns to this journal in our issue of February 8, 1913, Driscoll wrote: "My match with Moran was my last appearance as a principal in a ring encounter, and for the future I must be classed with the once-upon-a-timers ... I may as well retire now, as in six or twelve months time. Defeat is certain to come to those who fight against age, for the prize-ring isn't good soil for growing 'evergreens,' and I've seen so many of "the best pass along the line during the past twelve years, it would be foolish for me to attempt to keep on fighting ... It may be hard to say 'goodbye' to the scene of so many old associations, but there's

nothing like doing it now."

When he wrote the above Driscoll would have said no to any proposition that he should have "just one more fight," and what a pity it is he changed his mind so long after having felt convinced that he had had enough of the ring! It may be that now he has "come back" and been beaten he feels his reputation doesn't matter, but it does, and no sportsman, I am sure, wishes him to risk another defeat.

Four months ago the Earl of Lonsdale, the President of the National Sporting Club, when speaking at the Eccentric Club, said, "I notice that Jim Driscoll, one of the greatest artists we have ever had, has returned to the ring, but if it is a matter of money I am sure we would rather subscribe for an annuity for him than that he should be defeated by an inferior boxer." That was a timely suggestion, but, unfortunately for Driscoll, nothing was done to raise a fund which would make it unnecessary for him to box again; but although it is a little late now to give Jim a testimonial, this, it is hoped, will keep him out of the ring in future. More than £2,400 has already been subscribed for the old featherweight champion, and it is anticipated that that sum will at least be trebled.

On Thursday night I had a brief chat with Driscoll, and asked him if he was really going to sue for another match with Ledoux. His reply was: "I suppose I had better give the game best, but feeling so sure I can beat the Frenchman, I would not like to turn down an offer to meet him again." Since last Tuesday Jim has been attending Professor Frank Matthews, the bone-setter, each day for treatment to his left thumb, which was injured before his bout with Ledoux, and he attributes his defeat to having to limit the power he put behind his left hand shots during the contest.

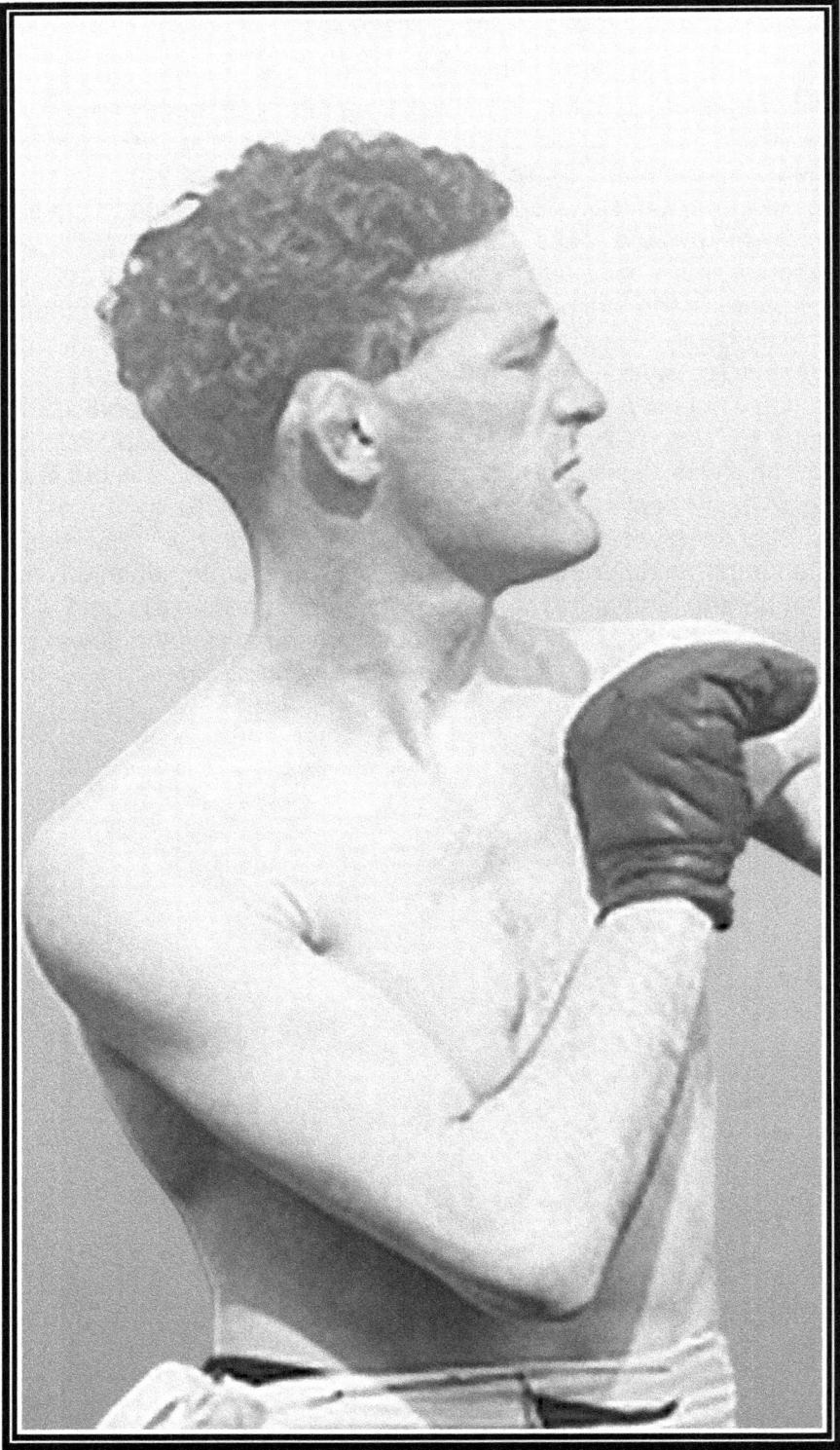

"AN OLD MAN MY LORD, A VERY OLD MAN!"

The Passing of Jim Driscoll

By Gerard Austin

When a somewhat grimy-looking towel flickered over the ropes and fluttered down into the ring in the opening seconds of the sixteenth round of the fight between Jim Driscoll and Charles Ledoux, there was hardly a man sitting round the squared circle at the National Sporting Club who didn't feel something rise up in his throat and choke him.

There is always something sad about a farewell - a long farewell to a great man's greatness, whether that *adieu* is uttered by a man staggering under a load of shame and obloquy, as was the former Cardinal Wolsey, or whether he is departing amid a blaze of glory, as was the case with that peerless fighter, the mighty Jim Driscoll.

Driscoll's finish was particularly sad, for the reason that one felt it had been quite unnecessary. Had the sporting world taken the same steps to relieve his urgent necessities before and not after his defeat by Charles Ledoux, the old lion could have remained in his den browsing upon the memories of a glorious past. But Dame Necessity is a stern taskmistress, a taskmistress to whom all must bow the knee willy-nilly, and Driscoll is no exception to the rule. Always the soul of free-thought of the rainy-day, in fact, even had he done so he could never have made any really adequate provision for his future, for in his most opulent moments Jim had never received a tithe of the money which second raters nowadays receive for performances which pale into insignificance before the achievements of the mighty little man from Cardiff.

A Man of Honor

As a fighter Jim was magnificent. As a man of business he was a failure. The competitive spirit he possessed in excess, the commercial was almost entirely absent from his make up. Jim's soul always scorned to grovel amid the yellow mud, the acquisition of which appears to be the be-all and end-all of the lives of most modern boxers. To him the sport was the thing. He took them as they came, and he took the money that was offered without haggling over either pelf or poundage. And it is that quality in his disposition which has earned him an imperishable niche in the affections of the sporting public. Throughout his long career the finger of suspicion was never pointed in his direction, and as a man of honour he ranks among the foremost of his kind.

Who will ever forget the sacrifice he made on the altar of honour in the winter of 1909? During the course of his visit to America in that year of grace he piled up a string of successes which has never been equaled let alone surpassed by any Englishman who has ever crossed the pond. The culmination, the crowning point of that wonderful tour, was his victory over Abe Attell, a victory so clear cut, so absolutely indisputable and decisive, that "Tad" (a fellow townsman of Abe Attell, and by no means a lover of things English) published a cartoon in the *Evening Journal* depicting Driscoll packing his grip with his right hand while he kept the Californian at bay with his long unerring left. Of course America went wild for Attell had hitherto been held to be invincible when on business bent. Offers poured in for Driscoll from Maine to California, from Chicago to New Orleans. Fortune could be his for the asking. And yet he refused the goods proffered by the gods and refused them without even a moment's hesitation.

Why?

Why just because he had promised that he would appear to box for the Nazareth House Charity in Cardiff, and all the gold in Ophir would not have been sufficient to induce him to go back on his plighted word. Is it any wonder then that people felt a lump rise in their throats as they saw that towel flicker into the ring and remembered that Driscoll, the idol of the modern ring, the beau ideal of what a boxer should be both in and out of the squared circle, had gone down to defeat battling for a few mangy quids which could have been his twice over had he remained in America and "loved not honour more"?

Jim as a Man

To the student of modern fistiana nothing is more striking than the tremendous improvement time, or something else, has wrought in the manners and behaviour of the knights of the padded glove. Thirty years ago and more some of the champion pugilists were by no means the civil and well conducted warriors of the more modern era. Glancing over a file of the *Sportsman* the other day, my eye was intrigued by the following priceless pearl of information:

> "New York, Saturday. Sullivan set upon and half killed a brakeman yesterday evening. The brakeman has been removed to hospital and Sullivan has been arrested."

A fine achievement to be recorded against a champion pugilist in very sooth. Our own champion, Charlie Mitchell, was also far from guiltless of this form of hooliganism, while I once saw a famous Australian pugilist strike an inoffensive little organ-grinder across the face with a Malacca cane. The fact that the little organ-grinder subsequently struck the big pugilist over the back of the head with a brick was a corollary which delighted all those who had been privileged to witness the cowardly assault of which the big fellow had been guilty. Even Jim Corbett - "Gentleman Jim" - was once guilty of the unpardonable offence of lifting under the jaw his stage manager, a gentleman who stood about 5' 1" in his boots!

In the person of Jim Driscoll has been reached the apotheosis of the gentleman and pugilist. A lion in the ring, a very lamb outside it. Driscoll's character might well be summed up in the farewell words of the old carpenter to Micah Clarke in Conan Doyle's great historical novel of that title:

> "Farewell then, Micah. Strong as a lion, tender as a woman, stern to the oppressor, gentle to the oppressed,

you have the esteem and love of all who know you."

Those words appear to me to fit the character of Jim Driscoll as does a hide a horse.

Jim as a Boxer

As a boxer, Jim Driscoll has ever combined under one hat all the qualities which go to make a champion among champions. It cannot be said of him that he was "first among equals," for in the days of his prime he had no equals, as he proved to demonstration time and time again. It is rare indeed that a boxer combines in his person all the talents. Generally there is a flaw - a tiny flaw - somewhere; there is one cog which mars an otherwise perfect mechanism. In Jim's fistic make-up there never has been a flaw. His generalship and ringcraft were as perfect as his defence. His timing and judgment of distance were as admirable as his hitting power, backed by that perfect leg-drive, was terrific. Nothing ever rattled him, no mishap was ever permitted to knock him out of his stride. Even in that first fight with Robson, when his breathing was clogged by a cold and his left eye was completely out of commission, he was always the consummate master of his art, watching with the only eye he could see out of for the chance he knew would come. There were some ugly moments during that fight, and many a champion I have seen would have gone down to dire and disastrous defeat. Perhaps the star of Jim's genious never shone so brightly as during those gloomy periods in the tenth and eleventh rounds.

The Triumph of the English Style

Always has the *Boxing World and the Mirror of Life* had a warm spot in its heart for Driscoll, if for no other reason than that he demonstrated many a time and oft that when practised by a master the English style will always beat the American, which latter is the very negation of fistic science as preached by the "B.W. and M.O.L" Driscoll wasn't the first to prove it, for Plimmer and others had done so, while Jim was in Knickerbockers, but Jim proved it

perhaps more decisively than any man before or since his time when he beat the head off Attell in New York. For when Driscoll met Attell, he encountered the man of all men in whom the American style reached it apotheosis, just as did in him the style inherited by the English school from the mighty Belcher. And Attell never saw the way Driscoll went. Even the American papers were unanimous upon the point, and I particularly remember one passage which occurred in the report of one of the leading fistic writers of New York.

> "In the eighth round the Attell contingent began rooting for a draw, a sure sign that they knew their man was los-ing, and this was rendered more obvious when right after the last round Attell jumped to the Press seats to ask who had won. Driscoll didn't worry - he knew!"

Can one wonder that the "B.W. and M.O.L.," with whom the cult of the English style has ever been a religion assumed a kind of fistic fatherhood to Jim of Cardiff and mourns his defeat as it might mourn the death of a well-beloved son?

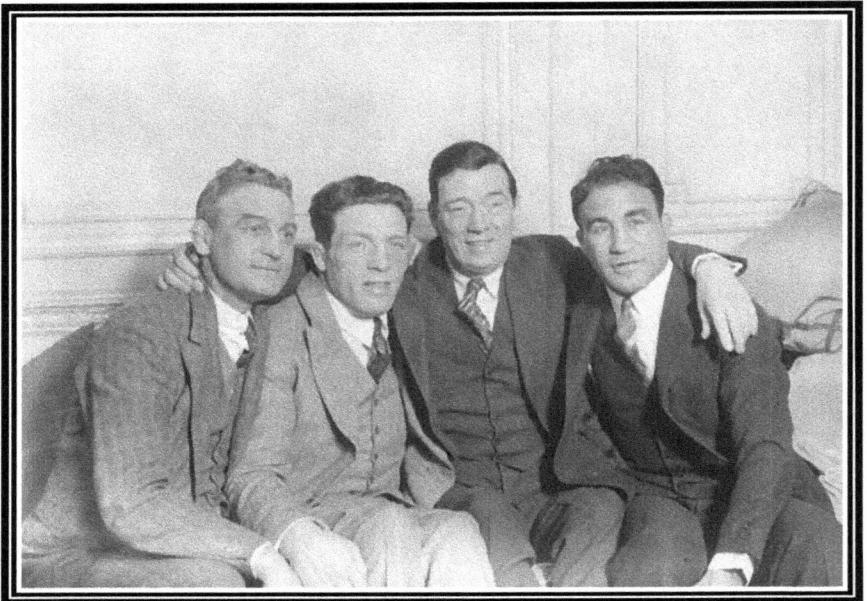

December 2, 1924. From left to right: Italian born American boxer Johnny Dundee, Jim Driscoll, Ted "kid" Lewis, and the man who managed them all, Jimmy Johnston.

The Law of Life

But, after all, why should we mourn? For nothing in all his fistic life became him like the leaving of it. What episode in his fistic history can compare with the last great stand of Jim Driscoll?

Not one that I know of, for there is none that merits even momentary comparison. The last stand of Jim Driscoll was Homeric, should be sung in epic verse, verse which should reverberate like thunder down the corridors of time. The tale of his passing should be printed in letters of gold and hung in a Hall of Heroes, there to be an example to the rising generations, for take him for all in all we may not look upon his like again.

Ever it is the same story, the story of life. Frogs and men are the same in all but form. The first year frog kills the second year frog, ultimately himself to become a second year frog and in his time pay the penalty of age. The old lion may have been king of the veld for years. He may have whipped rival lions innumerable and by sheer prowess of teeth and claw have monopolized to his own use the comeliest females of his tribe. But the day comes inevitably when the old champion of the felines is on the slide. His teeth decay and his thews refuse any longer to answer the mandates of the brain. And then it is that one of the younger males of the species pulls him down and rends them and then, over the carcase of his foe, roars his defiance to the world.

And the law of the jungle is the law of the ring. Always there are youngsters pushing their way to the front hustling the old 'uns down the dark corridors of defeat. And ever behind them are more youngsters clambering their way to the victory over the bodies of those who but yesterday were youngsters even as themselves. Youth will be served, for youth is nature who plays the game of life with the dice-cogged and who, therefore, always wins. Who was it wrote; "For Youth is ever youthful. It is only Age that grows old"? Whoever it was he knew whereof he wrote.

Driscoll - The Last Phase

It is curious to reflect what a curious fatality seems inevitably to overtake these six-year comebacks. Jackson quitted the ring in 1892 to return in 1898 to receive his quietus from the white man -

Jeffries. Jeffries in his turn left the ring in 1904 top return in 1910 to go down to defeat at the hands of Johnson, who thus avenged his brother black's defeat. Driscoll retired in 1913 to come back to defeat in 1919. But there is a great difference between these three famous comebacks, for whereas Jackson made no show with Jeffries and Jeffries went down to defeat in shame and dire disgrace, the last stand of Jim Driscoll will live for ever in fistic history. In days to come men now young, who will then be old, will tell their children how "An old man, me Lord, a very old man," whose favourite weapon was practically disabled, and who not long before had risen from a bed of sickness, entered a ring to defend the honour of England against an invader in the very prime of life and twelve years younger than himself. And they will tell, and tell truly, how the old lion battered and clawed and ripped his presumptuous adversary. And they will go on to tell how the old lion was conquered not by his adversary, the would-be usurper of the lordship of the jungle, but by youth, the invincible, the ever-unconquerable.

Hail to thee then, Jem Driscoll, of Cardiff, perhaps the greatest of all the Jems; of a surety by far the most iridescent gem which sparkles in the treasure chest of modern fistiana! Hail to thee, "Gem" Driscoll! Hail - and Farewell!

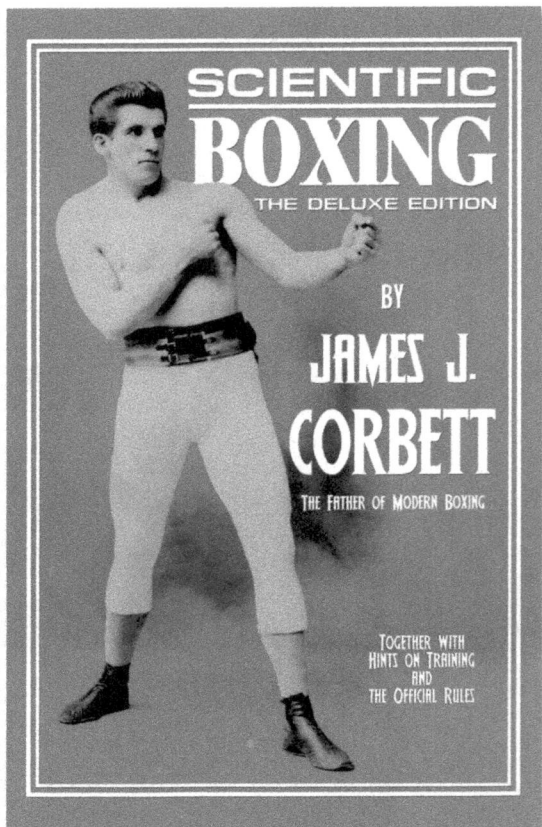

www.ingramcontent.com/pod-product-compliance
Lightning Source LLC
Chambersburg PA
CBHW060548100426
42742CB00013B/2491